Farm Woodland Practice

Edited by B.G. Hibberd
Research Communications Officer,
Forestry Commission

Prepared in co-operation with:
The Ministry of Agriculture, Fisheries and Food
The Department of Agriculture and Fisheries for Scotland
The Department of Agriculture for Northern Ireland
The Welsh Office Agriculture Department

LONDON: HER MAJESTY'S STATIONERY OFFICE

HMSO BOOKS

HMSO publications are available from:

HMSO Publications Centre
(Mail and telephone orders only)
PO Box 276, London, SW8 5DT
Telephone orders 01-622 3316
General enquiries 01-211 5656
(queuing system in operation for both numbers)

HMSO Bookshops
49 High Holborn, London, WC1V 6HB   01-211 5656 (Counter service only)
258 Broad Street, Birmingham, B1 2HE   021-643 3740
Southey House, 33 Wine Street, Bristol, BS1 2BQ   (0272) 264306
9–21 Princess Street, Manchester, M60 8AS   061-834 7201
80 Chichester Street, Belfast, BT1 4JY   (0232) 238451
71 Lothian Road, Edinburgh, EH3 9AZ   031-228 4181

HMSO's Accredited Agents
(see Yellow Pages)
and through good booksellers

ISBN 0 11 710265 2

ODC 26 : 913 : (410)

Keywords: Farm forestry

Acknowledgements

This Handbook *Farm woodland practice* and the companion publication Forestry Commission Bulletin 80 *Farm woodland planning* have been prepared in co-operation with the agricultural agencies listed on their covers, and with guidance and advice from many other sources including:

The Countryside Commission (England and Wales)
The Countryside Commission for Scotland
The Game Conservancy
The National Farmers' Union
The National Farmers' Union (Scotland)
The Nature Conservancy Council.

The principal authors are Forestry Commission officers working at the Forest Research Station, Alice Holt Lodge, near Farnham, Surrey (with the exception of Mr S. Bell who is based at the Forestry Commission's headquarters in Edinburgh). Those responsible for preparing individual chapters are as follows:

Chapter
1   Mr Brian G. Hibberd
2   Mr Huw L. Davies
3   Mr Huw L. Davies
4   Mr Mark J. Potter
5   Mr Donald A. Thompson
6   Mr Harry W. Pepper
7   Dr Hugh F. Evans, Dr John N. Gibbs
8   Dr Philip R. Ratcliffe
9   Mr Simon Bell
10 Mr Huw L. Davies
11 Mr Huw L. Davies

Thanks are also due to the many other Forestry Commission officers who have assisted in the preparation of this Handbook. Photographs are from the Forestry Commission collection.

Enquiries relating to this publication should be addressed to the Technical Publications Officer, Forestry Commission Research Station, Alice Holt Lodge, Wrecclesham, Farnham, Surrey GU10 4LH

Contents

Foreword

This Handbook covers the technical aspects of how to grow trees and woods and forms a companion volume to Forestry Commission Bulletin 80 *Farm woodland planning* which centres on management and economic aspects of farm woodlands. Sound technical knowledge is essential if planting and maintenance of woods are to succeed and this Handbook aims to satisfy this need by providing practical and comprehensive advice on how to carry out all operations concerned with woodlands grown on farms.

G J Francis
Director General
Forestry Commission

May 1988

1 The farm woodland initiative

The aim of this Handbook is to provide information about establishing, managing and harvesting trees on farmland. It explains and describes forestry techniques and systems suitable for use on the farm. The companion publication, Forestry Commission Bulletin 80 *Farm woodland planning*, provides details of costs, grants, income and regulations. Together, these publications form a comprehensive guide for those planting and managing farm woodlands.

The move towards planting trees on better land springs from changes in agricultural policy made necessary by agricultural surpluses. There is no likelihood of timber surplus in the United Kingdom, as even the most optimistic forecasts of production estimate no more than 30 per cent self-sufficiency in wood and wood products arising from the existing forestry area. Only 10 per cent of the United Kingdom's total land area of 24.1 million hectares has tree cover, compared with the EEC average of 25 per cent. The EEC is a net importer of wood and wood products and is likely to remain in that position in the foreseeable future.

Against this background the Government encourages the establishment of new woodlands by means of the Woodland Grant Scheme. Payments under the Farm Woodland Scheme are available in addition to grants under the Woodland Grant Scheme when under certain conditions land is being taken out of agriculture and devoted to woodlands. Current details of these schemes can be found in *Farm woodland planning* and in tree leaflets produced by the Forestry Commission and the Agriculture Departments (MAFF, DAFS, DANI and WOAD). Very small areas of planting such as hedgerows and field corners are not eligible for these schemes, and where such small plantings are contemplated the reader is directed to contact the Countryside Commission, the Countryside Commission for Scotland, the Tree Council or the local authority, as financial aid may be available through these bodies (see Appendix for addresses).

Although forestry schemes are not subject to planning permission, consultation with the Agriculture Departments, local planning authorities and other statutory authorities is necessary to ensure that the implications for agriculture, amenity, recreation and nature conservation are taken into account before approval is given for grant aided planting or for felling. The aim in this is to reconcile any conflict of views that might arise between the applicant and such authorities. The felling regulations referred to arise from the fact that, with certain exceptions, it is an offence to fell growing trees without first having obtained a licence from the Forestry Commission. Details can be found in the free booklet *Control of tree felling* issued by the Forestry Commission. Felling licences are not required in Northern Ireland.

The Farm Woodland Scheme enhances the financial incentive to establish new woodlands, being payable in addition to assistance received under the Woodland Grant Scheme (acceptance within which is a condition of entry to the Farm Woodland Scheme). To qualify for the Farm Woodland Scheme, the land must be in agricultural production (usually arable or improved grassland) and a minimum of 3 hectares (1 hectare in Northern Ireland) per holding must be planted over a 3-year period. The main aim of the Farm Woodland Scheme is to assist in taking land out of agricultural production. Not only is it intended that timber will be grown but also that the landscape will be enhanced and new wildlife habitats created. Where appropriate, new opportunities for recreational use and tourist interest may be sought. Not least of the Government's aims is that of supporting rural employment and farmers' incomes by worthwhile investment in trees on farmland.

New plantings of trees on land coming out of agriculture will vary from relatively small areas which, because of shape, position or landform, are difficult or awkward to cultivate or which produce only poor crops, to larger areas on which more traditional forestry patterns will be established. Whatever the size, shape or location of the woodland it will be essential to make the correct choice of species to meet the owner's requirements. In agriculture a poor choice of crops has only a short-term effect which can be corrected the following year. It is self-evident that tree crops which are unsuitable in a particular location or for a particular purpose will at best yield a poor return at the end of the day, and at worst constitute a continual drain on resources as, over the years, attempts are made to maintain the crop in the face of damage arising from the trees' inability to cope with their environment. The correct choice of species is, therefore, the most important decision that the prospective planter has to make. Where there is uncertainty about the end use for the trees planted, or a conflict of interests (wood production versus game for example), the correct choice will be for those species most likely to grow quickly and healthily in the location being considered.

Unlike most of the rest of Europe, where woodlands are often seen as a natural and integral part of farm management, Britain has virtually no tradition of farm forestry. In the absence of first-hand experience, some farmers in Britain may have gained the impression that forestry as a commercial activity is at odds with a caring attitude to the landscape and wildlife. They may also imagine that farm woodlands managed for conservation cannot be profitable. Indeed, it may appear to them that they are faced with only two options under the Farm Woodland Scheme; either commercial plantations which produce little other than wood, or some sort of nature conservation programme with little or no prospect of cropping. These misconceptions have to be dispelled if the Farm Woodland Scheme is to be successful and one of the chief aims of this Handbook is to describe and explain woodland systems which can achieve a variety of objectives according to the farmer's wishes.

2 Planning for farm woodland

Objectives

There are many reasons for planting trees on farms and the balance of these objectives should be considered carefully in planning new woodland so as to make the best choice of management system and species. It is important to consider all the major objectives; timber production, landscape, conservation, sport, recreation, shelter and minor products, because if one objective alone is followed, opportunities could be missed which may become more important as the woodland matures. It should be remembered that the choices made at the planting stage are likely to have a major effect on the use, attractiveness and profitability of the woodland for at least the first rotation of trees.

Once objectives have been finalised, it is sensible to set them out in a way similar to that of a farm management plan. Such a management plan should contain a list of intentions or objectives, prescriptions for achieving these and a record of work done.

There are two main systems of growing trees, high forest (this is what is usually considered as woodland or forest, single stemmed trees capable of growing to a large stature) and coppice (this is a crop raised from shoots produced from the cut stump of the previous crop – see Chapter 11), and these each suit particular objectives better than others.

Timber production

Timber production can mean anything from producing firewood and stakes for use on the farm, to producing high quality timber for joinery and veneers. It is essential to consider the type of timber to be produced, the time to reach marketable size and the potential markets. (Marketing timber is discussed in Chapter 5.) In most cases, both quality and quantity of material have to be considered in choosing the species and spacing to be adopted. The price of standing timber can vary widely from year to year (see Figure 2.1), so it is important to be flexible in the timing of operations producing substantial volumes of timber. In general, the larger the diameter of material the higher the price per unit volume (see Figure 2.2), but quality will always attract a premium, particularly in broadleaves. Some specifications for various markets are presented in Table 2.1. The smaller diameter specifications are often produced from conifer thinnings and the tops and branchwood of mature broadleaves and broadleaved coppice. Timber for several different markets may come from the same tree. In upland areas and on less fertile lowland sites conifers will almost certainly give a better return and the production of quality hardwoods in these areas is extremely unlikely. On sheltered, fertile lowland sites there is a much wider range of species that can give an acceptable return, and top quality broadleaved timber can only be produced from these sites.

Landscape

Trees and woods are very prominent features in the landscape and their changing effect is often seen by many generations. Both tree planting and tree felling change landscapes which have become familiar to one generation and so care is needed and landscape design should be an important consideration at all stages. Planting new woodlands or managing existing woods to enhance their role in the landscape should not be seen as an alternative to management for timber production, sport or other use, but as a complementary objective. The main factors affecting the landscape value of woodlands are the size and shape of the woodland, its species and its structure. These all interrelate with the agricultural landscapes surrounding them, particularly field size and boundaries – see Chapter 9.

The size and shape of a woodland should be in scale with the local landform and existing landscape of an area. In large-scale, open countryside with far reaching views, large blocks of woodland are appropriate, and small, scattered blocks can break up the scene and be distracting. In small-scale landscapes, where only small sections of countryside can be seen from any

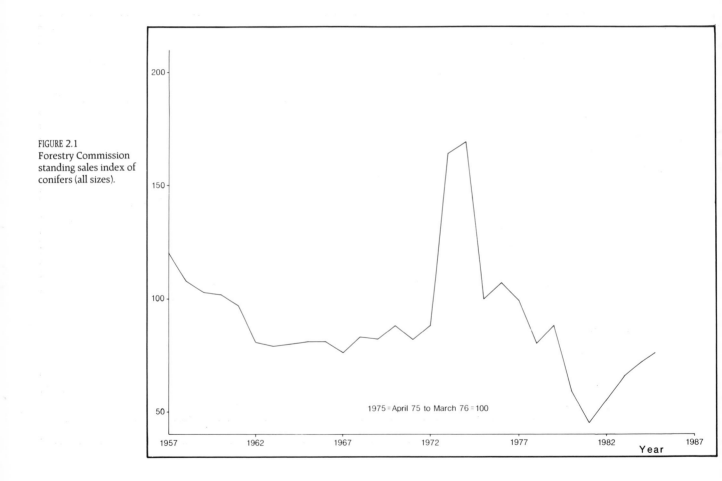

FIGURE 2.1
Forestry Commission
standing sales index of
conifers (all sizes).

1975 = April 75 to March 76 = 100

Year

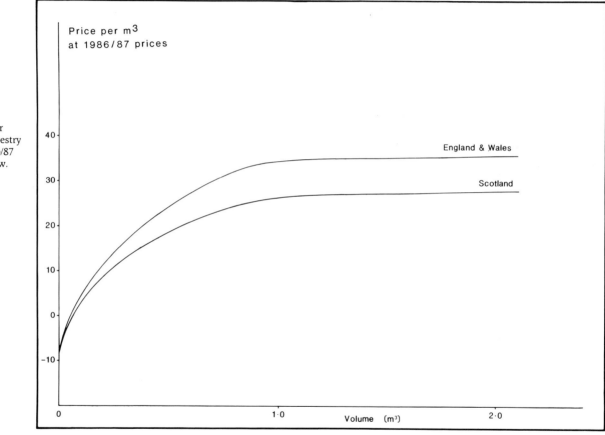

FIGURE 2.2
Price-size curves for
conifers for the Forestry
Commission's 1986/87
quinquennial review.

Price per m^3
at 1986/87 prices

England & Wales

Scotland

40

30

20

10

0

-10

0

1·0

2·0

Volume   (m³)

Table 2.1 Diameter specifications for various end-uses
Preferred ▬▬▬▬ and acceptable • • • • • •

Product	Diameter overbark (cm)						Comments
	10	20	30	40	50	60+	
Firewood	▬▬▬▬▬▬	▬▬	• • •				Hardwoods preferred
Pulpwood	▬▬▬▬▬▬	▬	• • •				Spruce and white hardwoods preferred
Turnery (ash/beech)	▬▬	▬▬	• • •				
(other broadleaves)	▬	• • •					
Fencing (round)	▬	• • •					Includes cleft chestnut
(sawn oak)		▬▬	▬▬	• • • •			
Mining timber (sawn)	▬	▬▬	• • •				Mainly oak
Sawlogs (conifer)	▬	▬▬▬	▬	•			
(hardwood)		• • • •	▬▬▬	▬	• • •		Only larger sizes of oak
Joinery (high class)		▬▬	▬	• • •			Mainly cherry and walnut
Veneer (ornamental)							
cherry/walnut		• • ▬	▬	• • •			
oak/elm				▬▬	▬	• • •	
other broadleaves			▬▬	▬▬	• • •		
Miscellaneous							
sports ash		▬▬	▬	• • •			
peeled poplar							
for crates		▬▬	▬▬	• • •			

viewpoint and the scene changes quickly on a route through the countryside, small woodland blocks are more appropriate. (The importance of size of woodland block in relation to cost of establishment must not be overlooked – see Chapters 4 and 6.) In flat landscapes, the size of plantation is not very important but the edges of the wood and its structure have a major effect. By structure is meant the relationship between unplanted bare areas, road, rides and crops of different heights or crown type, giving different landscape textures. The structure of the woodland becomes much more important if the viewpoints are close to the woodland, and is the dominant factor for landscape within the woodland.

The major factor of landscape importance in species choice is whether the species are evergreen or deciduous. In exposed situations or at high elevation, where conifers are likely to dominate any planting, the larches can be used to good effect as a deciduous element. It is important to remember that trees, like agricultural crops, change during the seasons; winter and summer views should be considered as well as autumn and spring colour.

Wildlife conservation

Any new woodland will create different habitats and attract new wildlife, and it is important to consider how existing wildlife communities will change and interact with surrounding areas. The effects of woodland design on wildlife are discussed in Chapter 8. Conservation interest can be enhanced by the use of native rather than exotic tree species (Table 2.2) and by creating and maintaining a diverse woodland structure.

Diversity in woodland structure can be achieved by having areas of coppice, a mix of deciduous and evergreen trees, the use

PLATE 1 Traditional woodland on steeper land with valley bottom retained for agriculture.

Table 2.2 Native species; trees generally accepted to be truly native, in approximate order of arrival

Common juniper	*Juniperus communis*
Downy birch	*Betula pubescens*
Silver birch	*Betula pendula*
Aspen	*Populus tremula*
Scots pine	*Pinus sylvestris*
Bay willow	*Salix pentandra*
Common alder	*Alnus glutinosa*
Hazel	*Corylus avellana*
Small-leaved lime	*Tilia cordata*
Bird cherry	*Prunus padus*
Goat willow	*Salix caprea*
Wych elm	*Ulmus glabra*
Rowan	*Sorbus aucuparia*
Sessile oak	*Quercus petraea*
Ash	*Fraxinus excelsior*
Holly	*Ilex aquifolium*
Common oak	*Quercus robur*
Hawthorn	*Crataegus monogyna*
Crack willow	*Salix fragilis*
Black poplar	*Populus nigra* var. *betulifolia*
Yew	*Taxus baccata*
Whitebeam	*Sorbus aria*
Midland thorn	*Crataegus laevigata*
Crab apple	*Malus sylvestris*
Wild cherry	*Prunus avium*
Strawberry tree	*Arbutus unedo*
White willow	*Salix alba*
Field maple	*Acer campestre*
Wild service tree	*Sorbus torminalis*
Large-leaved lime	*Tilia platyphyllos*
Beech	*Fagus sylvatica*
Hornbeam	*Carpinus betulus*
Box	*Buxus sempervirens*

of shrub species on woodland edges and maintaining open areas within the woodland. Wildlife value is also increased by retaining open areas next to stream sides, and by not draining and planting wet areas, but letting a marsh/bog community develop, or by creating ponds. Many features which improve conservation interest also increase the sporting potential of woodlands.

Recreation

Recreation needs to have a defined place in the list of objectives, so that decisions on planting and management can take account of present and possible future recreational needs. Public or private recreation may already take place on the site, along statutory rights of way, footpaths or bridleways. (Most timber producing species of conifer and broadleaves produce an attractive environment for walking, picnicking, etc., in older forest, and the best sites have a variety of species and ages of trees with some open areas.)

The main sporting use, particularly in lowland arable areas, will be pheasant shooting, though roe deer stalking may be important locally. Sporting use may be a very important objective and the design of woodland for this and control of damaging populations of some mammals is discussed in Chapter 6. The main requirements in choosing species appropriate to sporting use are the provision of a boundary hedge, typically hawthorn, blackthorn or holly, the inclusion of some conifers for winter warmth and the use of berry producing shrubs as sources of food. Berry producing shrubs, such as hawthorn, blackthorn or viburnum can also be useful as areas of low cover at flushing points (see Chapter 6).

Minor products

Minor products is a term used by foresters to describe any non-timber woodland products which are sold in small quantities. The most common minor products are foliage, Christmas trees, pea and bean sticks, and seeds. Foliage species are frequently grown as a mixture with crop trees, often with the intention of removing the minor product tree before it interferes with the crop tree, or growing it as an understorey on a coppice system. Christmas trees are better produced in an intensive nursery system (see Chapter 11).

Shelter

The provision of shelter can be considered in both stock rearing and arable areas. In arable areas, strips of woodland act as shelterbelts, and cut down windspeed if correctly designed. It is, however, necessary to look at shading effects on adjacent crops. In stock rearing areas, particularly in the Disadvantaged Areas (LFAs), the provision of woodland shelter for overwintering stock is often important. However, it is prudent in these circumstances to recognise when stock are likely to damage the trees by bark stripping or soil compaction, and analyse the objectives accordingly (see Chapter 6).

Choice of Species

Once the objectives have been set, species can be chosen to meet these requirements best for the given site. And within any one species a particular provenance or origin (see below) may be desirable. The main factors influencing how well any species will grow on a site are soil, climate and topography. In this Handbook, advice on choice of species is based on experimental evidence relating to a wide range of species and varieties grown throughout Britain.

Provenance and seed origin

Tree species which occur naturally over wide geographic ranges develop sub-populations with slightly different characteristics related to their local climate (e.g. altitude and day length). These populations are usually not visually distinguishable from one another, but each is slightly better suited to a particular environment. The term *origin* is used to describe the original native location of the seed of the trees. The term *provenance*, on the other hand, describes the place where the trees grew from which seed has been collected to produce new plants. Thus Douglas fir seed from trees on Vancouver Island is described as having that origin, while trees grown in Perthshire from that seed would produce seed of Perthshire provenance. Generally, origin is more important than provenance in chosing planting stock, and further information can be found in Forestry Commission Bulletin 66 *Choice of seed origins for the main forest species in Britain*. (Where origin is particularly important this is noted under the individual species in Chapter 3.)

Native and exotic species

Native species are those that colonised Britain unaided after the last Ice Age about 10 000 years ago. There are some 30 native tree species and many more native woody shrub species (see Table 2.2). Most of the major broadleaved timber trees are native, and these are particularly well suited where conservation as well as timber production is important. There are only three native conifer species, Scots pine, yew and juniper, and of these, only Scots pine is an important timber tree although yew can produce valuable wood. Some species are not native to the whole of Britain and, ideally, where conservation is a priority, it would be desirable to encourage native trees and shrubs within the exact limits of their natural distribution. This would assist in the maintenance of national diversity and regional character.

Because our climate is generally favourable to tree growth, a wide range of exotic tree species have been grown in Britain, and most of our major coniferous timber trees are exotic, generally from the north-west coast of America. There are few exotic broadleaves of importance in Britain although sycamore, sweet chestnut and English elm, have all become naturalised in Britain. The main recent introductions which may become more widely used are the southern beeches (*Nothofagus* species).

Timber production in Britain is concentrated on a very few species and this has obvious advantages when selling into a timber trade that is used to them. Because many plantations are concentrated on high ground and poor soils, there is a predominance of conifers, and particularly Sitka spruce, Scots and lodgepole pine. On more fertile lowland sites, high quality broadleaved timber can be grown and it is expected that a greater percentage of broadleaves will be planted in farm woodlands.

Soils

A wide choice of species exists for new farm woodlands on better soils in relatively sheltered conditions. A simple subdivision into soils with well aerated subsoils, poorly aerated subsoils, limestone soils and organic soils, will provide a good basis for species choice and the establishment techniques to be used. Table 2.3 shows a classification of soil types which can be used in conjunction with Table 2.4 (species choice) to produce a list of possible species which should grow well on farmland.

On brown earths, clays and loams a wide range of species will grow well, and the deciding factor for maximising timber production may be rainfall and the risks of summer drought or winter waterlogging. Most broadleaved species will grow in the uplands but unless the site is very sheltered then high quality

Table 2.3 Soil types for woodland planting

1. *Soil with well aerated subsoil*
   a. **Brown earths**
   Well drained predominantly loamy soils of relatively uniform brownish layers.

   b. **Sands, gravels and podzols**
   Very freely draining coarse textured soils liable to drought in areas of low rainfall. Podzols are predominantly sandy and sandy loam soils with a peaty surface layer overlying a pale, bleached sandy layer above a richly coloured orange or brownish soil. Podzols occur mainly in northern Britain and on sandy heaths in the south.

   c. **Ironpans**
   An ironpan is a thin, hard continuous layer in the soil where iron and manganese have been deposited and which presents a barrier to root development and the downward movement of water.

2. *Limestone soils (calcareous)*
   These are soils with a high lime content such as soils formed directly over chalk and limestones as well as some clays.

   a. **Free draining shallow soils**, e.g. Cotswolds.

   b. **Heavy soils**, e.g. Chalky Boulder Clays and Lias Clays.

3. *Soils with poorly aerated subsoils* (less than 50 cm peat) including all other clay soils not covered in 2b above.
   a. **Soft mineral soils**
   Ground water gleys with water rising from below but where draining is capable of achieving significant improvements within the rooting zone.

   b. **Peaty gleys** (less than 50 cm peat)
   These are very poorly drained waterlogged soils with an organic (peaty) surface layer, frequently occurring in areas of high rainfall.

   c. **Surface water gley**
   Heavy textured soils, wet from the surface which are improvable only with difficulty. In agricultural use, major investment in drainage is required before these soils can be cultivated. These are often soils in which the water table is very close to the surface.

4. *Organic and peatland soils (more than 50 cm peat)*
   a. **Grassy, flushed or herb-rich bogs**
   This group includes:
      i. *Molinia* (purple moor grass) and *Juncus* (rush) dominated **peat** bogs in areas of high rainfall.
      ii. Flushed bogs – which tend to develop on gentle slopes where water moves horizontally through the soil, e.g. the flushed peats of western Scotland and Wales. These **peats** are often of higher nutrient status than basin bogs.
      iii. **Fen peat** – formed in low lying areas under the influence of excessive or stagnant ground water. It may occur in areas with relatively low rainfall, e.g. East Anglian Fens, Somerset Levels and Lancashire Lowlands. Fen peats are typically rich in nutrients.

   b. **Unflushed basin bogs**
   Uplands, lowland and raised bogs formed under the influence of high ground water. These are very deep, soft **peats** usually dominated by sphagnum moss. These peats are of very low nutrient status.

   Blanket bog (Hill peat) – relatively firm **peat**, over 50 cm deep, e.g. bog peats occurring in areas of high rainfall such as Wales, the Pennines, Northern Ireland and Scotland. Typified by cotton grass and heather.

timber is unlikely to be produced, and broadleaves should be treated mainly as components to increase the diversity for landscape and wildlife conservation reasons. Birch, sycamore and alder are particularly important broadleaves in the uplands.

Climate and topography

The main climatic and topographic influences on species choice are rainfall, altitude and exposure, frost and winter cold. In general, as altitude increases yields decrease, but in some species this decrease is so large that the species would no longer produce an economic crop of timber. Exposure has the same effect as altitude and the outside 'edge trees' in a woodland are often shorter, more heavily branched and produce poorer timber than trees inside the woodland which benefit from mutual shelter.

Rainfall has little effect on the choice of broadleaved species but a considerable effect on conifers. In general, Corsican pine should not be planted in the wetter upland areas of the north and west owing to the increased chance of disease problems (see Chapter 7). In contrast, Douglas fir and Sitka spruce should not be planted in areas with very low rainfall and will grow better in the wetter west. Rainfall is the main reason for the good growth of Douglas fir on sheltered brown earth sites in the west, and Corsican pine on similar sites in the east.

Summer warmth is important for some species, notably walnut, sweet chestnut and black poplar hybrids; these should be confined to southern Britain. Spring frost is a particular problem in the early establishment of many species both broadleaved and conifer, and winter cold can restrict the planting of southern beech (Nothofagus) and eucalyptus species. In conifers, Norway spruce is particularly frost tolerant as is common alder in the broadleaves. One way of minimising frost damage on young broadleaves is to plant in mixture with conifers.

Mixtures

In many parts of Britain it has been traditional to plant broadleaves in mixture with conifers. There are many benefits from using mixtures but there can also be management problems. One of the main advantages of broadleaved/conifer mixtures is earlier financial returns. Owing to long rotations and slow growth of many broadleaves, a matrix of a faster growing species which matures sooner and brings earlier income may improve overall profitability. On exposed or frosty sites, conifers are used to 'nurse' broadleaves through the difficult early establishment stage. On most sites, growth of broadleaves in mixture with conifers is superior to that of a pure crop and will often produce taller, straighter stems on the broadleaves.

It is very important to ensure that the species mixed are compatible, and that both species are satisfactorily established through good weeding and cleaning. If mixtures are not compatible, one species will tend to dominate, often suppressing the other and negating any physical and consequent financial gains. On moist, fertile lowland sites, the conifer species, if wrongly chosen, can quickly outgrow the broadleaves, thus a mixture of slow growing beech with fast growing Douglas fir on such ground will lead to loss of the beech. On some high pH sites, the broadleaved component can dominate and suppress the conifer. Generally, when deciding on broadleaved/conifer mixtures, the expected conifer rate of growth should never be more than double that for the broadleaved component.

Some mixtures which have worked well on suitable sites are:

Oak with Norway spruce on heavy acid clays
Oak with European larch on lighter loams and alkaline clays
Oak with Scots pine on freely draining soils
Oak with ash and cherry on good brown earths or clay over chalk (these are usually laid out with groups of five oak at 12–15 m spacing, with lines of ash and cherry)
Ash with European larch or Norway spruce, with Norway spruce being used on wet sites and European larch on drier sites
Ash with oak and cherry
Ash with sycamore and sweet chestnut
Beech with Lawson cypress, western red cedar, European larch, Scots and Corsican pine
Beech with cherry
Japanese larch with Scots or Corsican pine

It is important that the mixture is as robust as possible to ensure survival of both species, and mixtures of three rows of broadleaves and three rows of conifers, or three rows of broadleaves and six rows of conifers are common for this reason. In undulating countryside, however, row mixtures can create very serious landscape problems with 'pyjama stripes'. One way of avoiding this problem is to plant in groups, with

Table 2.4 Species choice for farm woodlands

Soil type	Sands and podzols	Ironpans	Brown earths	Soft mineral soils (Acid clays)	Fen peats
		NON CALCAREOUS			
Occurrence	Lowland heaths and northern Britain	Mainly lowland heaths	Brown/red soil mixed farming areas	Mainly clay vales	Low lying fenland
Major broadleaved species	Birch Sweet chestnut *Nothofagus*	Oak Beech Birch *Nothofagus* Sweet chestnut Alder	Oak Ash Beech Sycamore Norway maple Poplar Sweet chestnut Cherry Alder Italian alder Willow Lime *Nothofagus* Walnut Hornbeam Birch	Oak Beech Sycamore Poplar Sweet chestnut Cherry Alder Willow Hornbeam	Poplar Sycamore Cherry Alder Willow
Major conifer species	Corsican pine Scots pine	Corsican pine Scots pine Douglas fir Larches	Corsican pine Scots pine Douglas fir Grand fir Noble fir Larches Sitka spruce Norway spruce Western red cedar Lawson cypress Western hemlock	Corsican pine Douglas fir Grand fir Noble fir Sitka spruce Norway spruce Western red cedar Lawson cypress	Corsican pine Douglas fir Larches Norway spruce

SOIL TYPE

	CALCAREOUS			UPLAND	
Free draining (Shallow soils less than 30 cm to rock)	Heavy (Well drained alkaline clays & brown earths)	Soft mineral soils (Alkaline gleys)	Brown earths	Surface water and peaty gleys	Peats
Typical soils of many chalk and limestone areas, e.g. Cotswolds	Chalk and limestone regions, especially on footslopes and valley bottoms	Low lying land often adjoining rivers and streams some clay vales	Upland valleys	Upland plateaux especially N.England S.Scotland & N. Ireland	Upland plateaux
Ash Beech Sycamore Norway maple Cherry *Nothofagus* Italian alder	Oak Ash Beech Sycamore Norway maple Poplar Cherry Lime *Nothofagus*	Oak Ash Beech Sycamore Poplar Cherry Alder Willow Lime	Oak Ash Beech Sycamore Cherry Alder Birch	Sycamore Alder Willow Birch	Alder Birch
Corsican pine Western red cedar Larches	Corsican pine Western red cedar Larches	Corsican pine Western red cedar	Corsican pine Scots pine Douglas fir Grand fir Noble fir Larches Sitka spruce Norway spruce Western red cedar Western hemlock	Lodgepole pine Larches Sitka spruce Norway spruce	Lodgepole pine Sitka spruce

groups of 12–25 broadleaves at 10–15 metre centres in a matrix of conifers.

The planting of mixtures of broadleaved species is uncommon, but most semi-natural woodlands have a wide mix of broadleaved species, and the inclusion of a small proportion of a second and third species in a plantation can benefit conservation and landscape. There is less of a problem with incompatability of growth rate in broadleaved mixtures, and these are often very successful.

It must always be remembered when planting small areas (less than 5 ha) that any timber produced must be sold in marketable units (see Chapter 5) and the use of mixtures or a wide range of species may bring management and marketing problems later in the life of the wood.

Further Reading

Forestry Commission publications

BULLETINS
14   *Forestry practice.*
62   *Silviculture of broadleaved woodland.*
64   *The yield of sweet chestnut coppice.*
66   *Choice of seed origins for the main forest species in Britain.*
80   *Farm woodland planning.*

BOOKLETS
15   *Conifers.*
20   *Broadleaves.*
44   *The landscape of forests and woods.*
50   *A key to eucalypts in Britain and Ireland – with notes on growing eucalypts in Britain.*

FOREST RECORDS
113 *Free growth of oak.*
122 *Nothofagus.*

HANDBOOK
2   *Trees and weeds.*

LEAFLETS
84   *Guide to upland restocking practice.*
85   *Windthrow hazard classification.*

88   *Use of broadleaved species in upland forests – selection and establishment for environmental improvement.*

OCCASIONAL PAPER
14   *The Gwent small woods project, 1979–84.*
17   *Farming and forestry.*

ARBORICULTURE RESEARCH NOTES
29/81/SILS *The native and exotic trees in Britain.*
33/81/EXT *The improvement of birch for forestry and amenity.*

MISCELLANEOUS
Practical work in farm woods. ADAS Leaflets P3017–P3024. MAFF/FC.

Other publications

ANON. *Wildlife conservation on the farm.* British Association for Shooting and Conservation.

ALLABY, M. (1983). *The changing uplands.* Countryside Commission Report CCP 153.

BECKETT, K. AND BECKETT, G. (1979). *Planting native trees and shrubs.* Jarrold.

BLYTH, J., EVANS, J., MUTCH, W.E.S. AND SIDWELL, C. (1987). *Farm woodland management.* Farming Press, Ipswich.

BROWN, I.R. (1983). *Management of birch woodland in Scotland.* Countryside Commission for Scotland.

COUNTRYSIDE COMMISSION (1983). *Small woods on farms.* Countryside Commission Report CCP 143.

EVANS, J. (1980). Prospects for eucalypts as forest trees in Great Britain. *Forestry* **53**(2), 129–143.

FAO (1980). *Poplars and willows in wood production and land use.* FAO Forestry Series 10. FAO, Rome. (328 pp.)

FINDLAY, D.C., COLBORNE, G.J.N., COPE, D.W., HARROD, T.R., HOGAN, D.V. AND STAINES, S.J. (1984). *Soils and their use in south west England.* Soil Survey Bulletin 14. Soil Survey of England and Wales, Harpenden.

GAME CONSERVANCY (1981). *Woodland and pheasants.* Game Conservancy Booklet 15. Game Conservancy, Fordingbridge.

HART, C.E. (1967). *Practical forestry for the agent and surveyor* (2nd edition). Estates Gazette.

MALCOLM, D.C., EVANS, J. AND EDWARDS, P.N. (eds.) (1982). *Broadleaves in Britain – future management and research.* Institute of Chartered Foresters, Edinburgh.

MORRIS, M.G. AND PERRING, F.H. (eds.) (1974). *The British oak – its history and natural history.* Published for the Botanical Society of the British Isles by E.W. Classey.

NATIONAL FARMERS' UNION (1986). *Farming trees – the case for government support for woodlands on farms.* NFU Policy Document.

PETERKEN, G.F. (1981). *Woodland conservation and management.* Chapman and Hall, London.

RACKHAM, O. (1976). *Trees and woodland in the British landscape.* J.M. Dent & Co., London.

SMART, N. AND ANDREWS, J. (1985). *Birds and broadleaves handbook.* Royal Society for the Protection of Birds, Sandy, Beds.

3 Individual species – characteristics, yield and use

In Britain, timber is generally measured and sold in cubic metres (m^3). The yield of timber over a rotation is measured in cubic metres per hectare per year over the rotation length and this is described as its yield class. For example, a stand of Yield Class 14 Douglas fir will produce an average of $14\,m^3\,ha^{-1}\,yr^{-1}$ for a rotation of 50 years. This yield will normally be spread over thinnings and final felling. Tables and graphs showing the usual pattern of yields throughout the rotation for stands of different yield class are available for use in FC Booklet 48. (Actual yield class can only be measured when trees are growing on a site, but estimates are often made for bare land based on the performance of species on adjacent land or similar soil and climatic types. Any given estimate of yield class will be for a particular species, and does not mean that other species will grow at the same rate on that site, e.g. a site producing Yield Class 14 Douglas fir might produce Yield Class 16 Sitka spruce or Yield Class 6 oak.) In the species descriptions below, the yield figures quoted are the range found in Britain, followed by the average in brackets. The averages are based on the whole of Britain and reflect the sites these species are grown on at present. Given fertile soils, sheltered conditions, correct matching of species to site and adequate establishment, yields from farm woodlands could be expected to be above the average for Britain. Yield is not the only factor affecting value, and particularly for broadleaved species, the quality of the timber is more important than yield. High quality oak logs can easily be ten times more valuable than poor quality logs of similar size.

Several broadleaved species can produce timber suitable for decorative veneers or high grade joinery if grown under the right conditions. Though specifications are exacting, the very high prices paid for this material mean that this market should not be ignored. Some species – notably cherry and walnut – can often be grown specifically for this purpose, but outstanding trees of most species can be sold to these markets. Identification and segregation of such stems at harvesting is always worthwhile.

Principal Broadleaved Species

Oaks: pedunculate oak, *Quercus robur* and sessile oak, *Quercus petraea*

British Isles and Europe

SITE
Well-aerated deep fertile loams. *Q. robur* grows well on fertile heavy soils and marls. Strong light demanders. Sessile oak tolerates less rich soils than does pedunculate oak.

Avoid all shallow, ill drained or infertile soils, and exposed areas. Timber liable to 'shake' on very free draining soils.

TIMBER
Oak is hard and resistant to abrasion. It has a naturally durable heartwood, but the sapwood needs preservative treatment when small poles are to be used out of doors. Prime clean oak might be suitable for veneers or planking for the furniture industry. Second qualities can be used for beams, flooring, fencing and temporary engineering. Lower grades of oak are used for sawn mining timber, pulpwood and firewood. Small poles are valued for cleft or round fence stakes.

YIELD
2–8(4)

REMARKS
Both species are very windfirm. Bark is still harvested as tanbark in southern England. Sessile oak is less prone to epicormic branching than pedunculate oak. On sites with fluctuating water tables, trees larger than 40 cm diameter may suffer from shake.

Beech, *Fagus sylvatica*

Southern England, south Wales and Europe

SITE

Tolerant of chalk and limestone soils. Good loams of all types if well drained. Likes a mild sunny climate. A good shade-bearer.

Avoid frost hollows, heavy soils on badly drained sites and leached soils.

TIMBER

Beech has a wider range of indoor uses than any other home-grown hardwood, but is rarely employed out of doors. It is strong, works well to a good finish, and is easily stained. Its uses include furniture, particularly for non-visible framing and in kitchens and schools, turnery, flooring, bentwood and pulpwood. It is a good wood for pallets, charcoal making and firewood.

YIELD

4–10(6)

REMARKS

Benefits from a nurse on exposed areas; Scots pine is a suitable species. Useful for underplanting. Grey squirrels can be very destructive to young beech. Stem form often poor. Dense planting gives better chance of selecting individuals for final crop.

Ash, *Fraxinus excelsior*

British Isles and Europe

SITE

A most exacting species which demands good soil conditions. Likes sheltered situations and deep calcareous loams, moist but well drained. Thrives on chalk and limestone but only where soil is deep. Benefits from shelter in youth. Not a suitable species for use on open ground.

Avoid dry or shallow soils, heath or moorland, ill-drained ground, heavy clays. Frost hollows and exposed situations are also unsuitable.

TIMBER

Ash has a high resistance to shock and is thus used for oars, hockey sticks and other sports equipment, vehicle framing, tool handles, turnery and furniture. However, ash with annual rings wider than 6 mm or smaller than 1.5 mm will be unsuitable for these purposes. Also used for pallets, pulpwood and firewood.

YIELD

4–10(5)

REMARKS

It is no use planting ash unless there is local evidence that first-class timber can be produced. It is necessary to choose these sites with great care.

Sycamore, *Acer pseudoplatanus*

Central Europe

SITE

Requires a moderately fertile freely drained soil, it is tolerant of calcareous soils. Fairly frost hardy. Stands exposure and smoke pollution very well. Avoid very dry or shallow soils, and ill-drained ground.

TIMBER

A white timber especially suitable for use in contact with food (kitchen utensils, butchers' blocks, bread board, etc.). A good turnery timber; used for textile rollers and bobbins. Figured sycamore is much sought after for veneer and furniture manufacture. Also for pallets, pulpwood and firewood.

YIELD

4–12(5)

REMARKS

A useful windfirm tree, suitable for mixture with conifers in shelterbelts. Grey squirrels can be very damaging. Capable of producing valuable timber in the uplands and on sites too poor for oak.

Norway maple, *Acer platanoides*

Northern and eastern Europe

SITE

Prefers a deep, moist soil, preferably alkaline. It will also tolerate less fertile and drier sites than will sycamore. It grows best on deep soils over chalk, but is one of the few species capable of growing well on the thin soils of chalk downland. Avoid exposed sites and frost hollows.

TIMBER

A white-grey wood with characteristics similar but slightly inferior to sycamore. Used for the same purposes as sycamore.

YIELD

Not enough grown to predict yield. Probably in the same range as sycamore.

REMARKS

A very useful tree, particularly on soils with a high pH. Grows faster than sycamore when young. Grey squirrels can be very damaging.

Sweet chestnut, *Castanea sativa*

Mediterranean

SITE

Needs a moderately fertile light soil, and it does best in a mild climate. Profitable as coppice in the south of England. Unsuitable for frosty or exposed sites, badly drained ground or alkaline soil.

TIMBER

Coppice-grown material is used for cleft fencing and hop poles. Sawn timber is used for furniture, coffin boards and as a general purpose substitute for oak.

YIELD

4–10(6)

REMARKS

One of the best species for farm woodlands in the south of Britain, producing first class fencing material on a coppice rotation and useful saw timber on longer rotations. Large size logs can be subject to shake, particularly on sites where water tables fluctuate each year.

Poplars: Black hybrids, *Populus × euramericana*

P. 'Eugenei', *P.* 'Gelrica', *P.* 'Heidemij', *P.* 'Robusta', *P.* 'Serotina'.

SITE

Very exacting; suitable sites are limited. Loamy soils in sheltered situations. Rich alluvial or fen soils, both well-drained and well-watered. Banks of streams. Avoid high elevation, exposed sites and shallow soils. Stagnant water is fatal but occasional floods do no harm. Avoid acid peats and heathland. Not suitable for northern and western Britain.

TIMBER

Large clean poplar is peeled for veneer. Also used for light boxes and crates, packaging, pallets, and fencing. High resistance to abrasion. Good pulpwood.

YIELD

4–14(6)

REMARKS

See Chapter 11.

Balsam poplars: *P. trichocarpa, P. tacamahaca × trichocarpa* hybrids

North America

SITE

Often susceptible to a bacterial canker and only clones generally resistant in practice should be used, e.g. *P. trichocarpa* 'Fritzi Pauley' and 'Scott Pauley' and the *P.* 'Balsam spire' (T×T 32). They withstand slightly more acid soils than the black hybrids and are more suited to the cooler and wetter parts of Britain. Avoid high elevation, exposed sites and shallow soils. Stagnant water fatal but occasional floods do no harm. Avoid acid peats and heathland.

TIMBER

Large clean balsam poplar has similar uses to the black hybrids.

YIELD

4–16(6)

REMARKS

See Chapter 11.

Wild cherry (gean), *Prunus avium*

British Isles and central Europe

SITE

Requires a fertile, deep, well drained soil which ideally should be slightly acid though it also does well on deep loams over limestone. It responds well to chemical weeding and to early thinning, and can be grown in the open. Avoid dry or shallow soils, ill drained ground and exposed situations.

TIMBER

Cherry timber has a rich reddish brown heartwood which is very rarely if ever shaken. It is suitable for turnery, furniture, veneers and decorative panelling.

YIELD

4–10

REMARKS

Best grown as groups in a mixture of broadleaves. Not often damaged by grey squirrels but suffers from bacterial canker and an aphid pest. Can produce very high value timber from farm woodland, particularly if heavily thinned and high pruned.

Walnut, *Juglans regia* and *Juglans nigra*

South-east Europe and Asia, and eastern North America

SITE

The ideal site is sheltered with a southerly aspect, and a moderately fertile, well drained soil of medium texture. pH should be near neutral (pH 6–7). Walnuts thrive in warm summers and their planting should be confined to southern Britain. Walnuts should be open grown or grown in small groups at 12–15 cm centres in mixed woodland. Pruning will be necessary to achieve a straight bole of 2–3 m, and should be done in July or August. Avoid very clayey or very sandy sites and frost hollows.

TIMBER

A grey or brown timber with streaks of darker colour, giving a very decorative finish. The wood is used for furniture and decorative joinery, usually as veneer. Other uses include rifle butts.

YIELD

Quality is much more important than quantity, and as walnuts are usually open grown as single trees or small groups, yield class is not usually estimated.

REMARKS

Both species are capable of producing high quality, decorative timber in southern Britain. *J. nigra* grows slightly faster than *J. regia*, but the timber may not be as highly figured.

Alder, *Alnus* species

British Isles, northern and southern Europe, North America

SITE

Mainly on poorly drained wet land, particularly acid clays, but grey alder and Italian alder tolerate dry conditions, making them useful for reclamation sites. Italian alder is capable of high yields and grows well on alkaline sites. All species do better in a sheltered position. Common alder is very frost hardy. Avoid very exposed sites and dry sites (except grey and Italian alder).

TIMBER

General purpose timber with a coarse texture, suitable for turnery, pallets, charcoal and pulp.

YIELD

4–13

REMARKS

All species coppice freely (except Italian alder) and all fix nitrogen, making them particularly useful in mixtures and on nutrient deficient sites.

Birch, *Betula pendula* and *Betula pubescens*

British Isles, northern Europe and Asia

SITE

Birch is rarely planted but regenerates naturally on almost any bare mineral soil in Britain. Open disturbed sites on light soils are best, but birch is capable of rapid growth on most sites. Stands frost and exposure very well.

TIMBER

Birch wood is white or pale fawn, only moderately dense and can be used for turnery, pallets, firewood and pulpwood.

YIELD
4–10

REMARKS
Birch coppices freely when young and is useful as a nurse crop in mixtures, but it must be kept under control or it will smother a slower growing tree crop. It may have a role as a soil improver on acid soils.

Willow, *Salix* species

British Isles, Europe

SITE
Willow is rarely planted for timber production in Britain, but is useful for conservation and amenity not only on wet soils near running water but also as a coloniser of unweathered material such as shale and coal waste. Cricket bat willow (*Salix alba* v. *coerulea*) is planted as a crop at wide spacing on deep fertile alkaline loams near running water in the south of England (see Chapter 11).

TIMBER
The only willow grown for timber is the cricket bat willow, reaching utilisable size in 12–18 years.

REMARKS
All willows coppice well and are useful for windbreaks, screening and possibly for biomass production. Cricket bat willow can suffer from watermark disease (see Chapter 7).

Southern beech, *Nothofagus procera* and *Nothofagus obliqua*

South America

SITE
Requires a moderately fertile sheltered site. Will grow on most soil types apart from shallow soils over chalk or on acid peats. Will generally produce good volume growth on sites regarded as marginal for ash or oak.

TIMBER
Both species produce a moderately dense, fairly strong wood which may be used for furniture, flooring, interior and exterior finishes, firewood and pulpwood.

YIELD
10–20 (12)

REMARKS
Careful attention should be given to provenance, as both species can suffer dieback and death as a result of extreme winter cold. The best stands in Britain have been raised from seed collection in the Chilean provinces of Cautin and Malleco, though recent provenance trials indicate that Argentinian seedlots can be markedly superior.

Hornbeam, *Carpinus betulus*

Europe

SITE
Grows well on damp clays and thrives on both acid brown earths and soils derived from chalk and limestone. A frequent component of coppice underwood in SE England. Very frost hardy and shade tolerant. Slow growing.

TIMBER
Very dense, hard timber. Specialised uses for turnery, wood carving and parts of musical instruments. Also good for charcoal and firewood.

YIELD
Insufficient information.

REMARKS
A useful component of coppice underwood, especially in parts of the country where it is native.

Lime, *Tilia platyphyllos* (large-leaved); *Tilia cordata* (small-leaved); *Tilia* × *europea* (common lime)

Europe

SITE
Both small-leaved and large-leaved lime require soils of high pH and are suited to both deep and shallow soils over chalk and limestone. Small-leaved lime coppices strongly and is a valued component of mixed broadleaved woodland and an understorey layer in shelterbelts. Large-leaved lime and common lime are

very large trees. Common lime is used extensively as a street and parkland tree for amenity. Not suitable for extensive planting.

TIMBER
A very soft, light, white or yellow timber of limited use. Mainly turnery and wood carving. Can be used for pulp and firewood but its low density is a disadvantage.

YIELD
Insufficient information.

REMARKS
Small-leaved lime is of high conservation interest in areas where it is native. Large-leaved lime and common lime are useful parkland trees where they can achieve considerable size.

Elm, *Ulmus* species

Because of Dutch elm disease, woodland planting of elm cannot yet be encouraged. However, many hedgerows show elm re-growth and this can be expected to survive for about 20 years and then succumb, to be followed by further regeneration.

Principal Conifer Species

Scots pine, *Pinus sylvestris*

British Isles and northern Europe

SITE
An adaptable tree which succeeds over a wide range of conditions. The easiest tree to establish on dry heather sites. Thrives on light or sandy soils and at low or moderate elevations. Very frost hardy. A strong light demander. Does well in low rainfall areas. A useful nurse species.

Avoid poorly drained ground and sites exposed to sea wind. Not easy to establish on moorland country under high rainfall. Unsuitable for chalk or limestone soils except as a nurse for beech.

TIMBER
A general purpose timber with good strength properties. It works, nails and finishes well. Takes preservatives readily so is easily treated for outdoor use. Its wide range of uses includes fencing, joinery, construction, oriented strand board, flooring, packaging, pallets, pitwood, fibreboard, chipboard manufacture and transmission poles. The 'redwood' of the imported timber trade.

YIELD
4–14(8)

REMARKS
Although growth is rather slow and volume production is not high compared with the more exacting species of pines, it is generally a 'safe' tree to plant. Use plants produced from seed orchard seed.

Corsican pine, *Pinus nigra* var. *maritima*

Corsica

SITE
Low elevations, particularly sandy areas near the sea. Light sandy soils and also heavy clays in the Midlands and south and east England; low rainfall areas. More successful on chalky soils than Scots pine. Tolerates smoke better than other evergreens.

TIMBER
The timber resembles that of Scots pine but is somewhat coarser in texture, has a higher proportion of sapwood, and is not quite so strong. Readily treated with preservatives. Its uses include construction, box manufacture, pitwood, fencing, fibreboard manufacture, pulpwood, transmission poles and wood-wool.

YIELD
6–20(11)

REMARKS
It is important to obtain plants of true Corsican provenance – that is plants raised from seed collected in Corsica, or their descendants. Though this species is more difficult to establish it produces timber faster than Scots pine.

Lodgepole pine, *Pinus contorta*

Western North America

SITE
After suitable ground preparation lodgepole pine grows relatively well on the poorest heaths, and peat where no other tree will survive. Stands exposure better than most other species. Fairly tolerant of air pollution. For optimum results, the choice of correct provenance is important. Tends to grow very coarsely on moist fertile sites.

TIMBER
Home-grown timber is used in the round for pitprops and fencing. The sawn timber has similar properties to Scots pine and can be used for the same purposes.

YIELD
4–14(7)

REMARKS
Is probably the best pioneer species in Britain and is now being widely planted, especially in the west and north. Coastal provenances generally have higher yield than inland provenances but are of poor form. Vulnerable to pine beauty moth in north Scotland. For pure stands, a combination of good form and high volume production can be achieved with provenances from Skeena River, Vancouver Island, and Southern Interior of British Columbia origins. For use in mixture with Sitka spruce, Alaskan or North Costal origins are most likely to produce a good nursing effect and lead to a final crop of pure spruce.

Japanese larch, *Larix kaempferi*

European larch, *Larix decidua*

SITE
Thrives over wide range of conditions, including the high rainfall districts of the west and north. Suitable for upland sites including grassy and heathery slopes. Of great value in coppice areas and, in the case of Japanese larch, in fire belts as it quickly outgrows and suppresses adjoining vegetation. A valuable pioneer species and useful nurse.

Avoid dry sites and areas where the annual rainfall is low (under 750 mm/30 inches); also badly drained sites, frost hollows and very exposed situations.

TIMBER
The timber is heavier and stronger than that of most other softwoods. The heartwood is naturally durable but any sapwood needs preservatives for outdoor use. It is widely used for fencing, gates, estate work and pitwood. Other uses include telegraph poles, rustic work, garden furniture, pallets and chipboard. Selected material is in demand for vat making, boat building, and wagons.

YIELD
4–16(8)

REMARKS
Japanese larch is resistant to larch canker. Gives a higher yield, up to middle age, than European larch or Scots pine. Seed from British plantations should be preferred. With European larch, canker is a problem, and the origin of seed is very important. Registered seed stands in Britain should be the first choice, with imports from the Sudeten area of Czechoslovakia and from low elevation plantations outside of its native range in Germany next. Not a high yielding species.

Hybrid larch, *Larix × eurolepis*

First raised in Scotland

SITE
Of special value on sites which are at the limits for the use of European or Japanese larch. Hardier and more resistant to disease. On good sites can grow even more quickly than Japanese larch. Shows some tolerance of smoke pollution.

Avoid dry sites and areas where annual rainfall is low (under 750 mm/30 inches); also badly drained sites, frost hollows and very exposed situations.

TIMBER
Resembles the timber of European larch and grade for grade can be used for much the same purposes.

YIELD
4–16(8)

REMARKS

Characteristics are intermediate between European and Japanese larch but depend on the particular parents of the hybrid. First generation hybrid from selected parents is outstanding; second generation hybrid is also valuable, but third generation is poor.

Douglas fir, *Pseudotsuga menziesii*

Western North America

SITE

Requires a well-drained soil of good depth and of moderate fertility. A tree for valley slopes. Particular care is needed in site selection. Can bear shade as a young tree for a few years. Unsuitable for exposed situations, heather ground, wet soil and shallow soils. Liable to windblow on soft ground except where drains are well maintained. Suffers from frost damage when young.

TIMBER

An excellent constructional timber with a high strength to weight ratio in compression and bending. Takes preservatives reasonably well. It can be used for fencing, pitwood, flooring, joinery, construction, packaging, pallets, telegraph poles, flag poles, chipboard, fibreboard and pulpwood.

YIELD

8–24(14)

REMARKS

On suitable sites Douglas fir grows rapidly and produces a high volume of timber. Thinning at too late a date can render crop unduly susceptible to windblow. Good drainage is important.

Norway spruce, *Picea abies*

Europe

SITE

Moist grassy or rushy land, and shallow, less acid peats. Succeeds on old woodland sites and most soils of moderate fertility including heavy clays. Can withstand light shade for a few years. Somewhat sensitive to exposure. Fails on heather land and does poorly on dry sites, particularly on eastern side of

Britain. May be checked by frost in hollows and by occasional grazing by roe deer and sheep, but eventually grows away from this.

TIMBER

A good general purpose timber with a clean white colour, which works and nails well, and has a wide range of uses. It is stable during changing conditions of humidity and is therefore particularly suitable for building. Its uses include joinery, packaging, pallets, pulpwood, chipboard, pitwood, fencing, fibreboard, ladder poles and scaffold poles. The 'whitewood' of the imported timber trade. Seldom used out of doors as the heartwood is hard to treat with preservative, but small poles take enough preservative in their sapwood to fit them for fencing.

YIELD

6–22(12)

REMARKS

Norway spruce produces a high volume of timber. Good drainage is essential if windblow is to be avoided. The young trees and tops of thinnings can be sold as Christmas trees. Choice of provenance is important. East European origins are generally best, except when growing specifically for Christmas trees, when origins from the Schwabische region of Germany are preferred.

Sitka spruce, *Picea sitchensis*

Western North America

SITE

Damp sites generally, especially exposed high land. Stands exposure better than any other common conifer, very suitable for high rainfall districts especially on the west coast. Avoid all dry sites. Honey fungus is a risk in some scrub and coppice areas. Not a tree for the dry east nor for southern and midland England. Can suffer severe damage from frost when young.

TIMBER

Properties and uses are slightly superior to those of Norway spruce. A first class pulpwood and readily accepted for chipboard, boxboards, packaging, pallets and carcassing jobs, but not for high grade joinery.

YIELD
6–24+(12)

REMARKS
A faster grower than Norway spruce and a very large volume producer. Wide provenance variation. Queen Charlotte Islands (BC) is a safe choice but on southern sites Washington and Oregon are preferred.

Western red cedar, *Thuja plicata*

North America

SITE
Requires a sheltered site with a deep fertile freely drained soil. It does better in the high rainfall areas of the south and west, but has also performed satisfactorily on thin soils over chalk. It is not too susceptible to frost. Its shade tolerance and narrow crown shape make it useful in mixtures. Avoid very dry sites.

TIMBER
A very light timber with a coloured heartwood which is extremely durable. Can be used as sawn timber for framing in greenhouses, seedboxes, gates and cladding on buildings. Also used for chipboard, pitwood and pulpwood.

YIELD
6–24(12)

REMARKS
A useful estate tree with uses as fencing when young, good in mixtures and useful cover for sporting woods. Especially good on alkaline soil. The best seed source is from the Olympic Mountains, Washington.

Lawson cypress, *Chamaecyparis lawsoniana*

North America

SITE
Requires a fertile brown earth soil for good growth, but can be successfully established on heavy clay sites. Prefers sheltered locations with moderate to high rainfall. It is a shade bearer, so can be used to underplant other crops or in mixture. Avoid frosty sites, dry and alkaline soils. Not good on exposed sites and may be subject to windblow on waterlogged sites.

TIMBER
Heartwood is resistant to decay, small poles can be used for fencing and mining timber, larger material provides general purpose saw timber.

YIELD
8–20(12)

Firs, *Abies* species

North America and Europe

SITE
The firs are capable of being grown on a wide variety of sites, but prefer well drained mineral soils. The grand fir (*Abies grandis*) is a very high volume producer in sheltered valleys, and the noble fir (*Abies procera*) is capable of withstanding severe exposure so could be more useful on upland areas. Both species do better in the moister west of the country than the drier east. Both species and several minor species can be used as Christmas trees. Most species establish very slowly and then grow rapidly.

TIMBER
Generally a white timber which is not durable but accepts preservative and works well to give a good finish. Its uses include for general estate use, mining timber, packaging, carcassing, chipwood, fibreboard and pulp.

YIELD
8–34(14)

REMARKS
The firs are useful species with remarkably fast growth rates on some sites. They are particularly useful on drier sites which are unsuitable for spruces. Seed origins of grand fir from the north of its natural range – Washington and Vancouver Island – are recommended.

Western hemlock, *Tsuga heterophylla*

Western North America

SITE

No well marked climate preferences. Does well in the west and may be highly productive in quite low rainfall areas. Acid mineral soils and the better peats. A strong shade bearer and excellent for underplanting. Most competitive with other shade bearers on dry brown earths. Rather difficult to establish pure on bare ground, and does better with a nurse. Sites where previous conifer crops have suffered from *Heterobasidion (Fomes) annosum* and *Armillaria mellea* should be avoided, as hemlock is prone to butt rot from these fungi.

TIMBER

Home-grown hemlock has good prospects as a building timber and – if graded for the purpose – as a joinery timber. Also for pitprops and general estate work. A good pulpwood.

YIELD

12–24+(14)

REMARKS

Is best established under some shade. Vancouver Island origins are good for most UK sites.

Further Reading

Forestry Commission publications

BULLETINS
14   *Forestry practice.*
62   *Silviculture of broadleaved woodland.*
66   *Choice of seed origins for the main forest species in Britain.*
75   *The silviculture and yield of wild cherry.*
77   *British softwoods: properties and uses.*

BOOKLETS
15   *Conifers.*
20   *Broadleaves.*
48   *Yield models for forest management.*

4 Establishing new farm woodland

Site Preparation

Most of the land that will be used for establishing new woodlands on farms will offer good conditions for tree growth and allow planting to be undertaken with a minimum amount of preparation work provided the site is not too wet. The extent to which work can be mechanised will depend on available machinery and the scale of operations. The following sections summarise the methods that might be used for a range of site types.

Arable land

A variety of operations can be undertaken to improve the conditions of the site into which the young tree is planted. The aim of such work is to provide a weed-free area of warm, drained and aerated soil.

Land that has been regularly cultivated will provide an ideal medium for planting trees. Such ground is likely to be of high nutrient status and initially weed-free, though rapid colonisation can be expected. It is unlikely that any substantial site preparation will be needed and it may be possible to adapt agricultural planting machines to cope with certain types of forest planting stock where the ground is reasonably level.

Where soils have been repeatedly cultivated for many years, it is possible that a 'plough pan' may have developed and, whereas this may not greatly affect shallow rooting farm crops, the growth rates of trees could be reduced and the woodland may become unstable in later years due to poor root development. Where there is evidence of such conditions the pans should be broken by deep cultivation.

Grassland

All types of pasture will be suitable for the establishment of trees provided that the grass around the base of each tree is killed over an area of at least 1 m diameter (see weed control section on p.36). If a site is wet the ground can be ploughed with shares set at 2–3 metres apart to combine initial weed control with the provision of a dry planting spot and a rudimentary drainage system.

Existing woodland

Existing woodland is not eligible for payments under the Farm Woodland Scheme.

Woodland of low productivity or poor stocking can be improved by enrichment (in which trees of more productive species or better stock are planted through the area) or group planting (to replace fallen or failed trees). In either case it is important to ensure that the newly planted trees are free from competition and receive sufficient light. When trees are planted at wide spacing, it may be uneconomic to fence the whole area to prevent deer damage: *treeshelters* (see page 35) are a cost-effective alternative in such cases.

Where felling has recently taken place, cut branches can hinder planting and weeding, and also harbour rabbits. The presence of branch material may be disregarded where the rabbit population is under control and sufficient access to planting spots is available. In other cases the problem should be dealt with at the harvesting stage, since windrowing or burning are normally too expensive to justify as separate operations (see also Chapter 10).

Clearance of trees will usually lead to a rise in the water table and this can create very boggy conditions. As well as making access across the site difficult, the wet conditions encourage invasion by vigorous grasses and can exacerbate the effects of frost. These problems are likely to be most severe on heavy clays where it will be better to delay timber extraction until the ground is frozen hard or at its driest in summer.

Planting Stock

Young trees are sold in a bewildering variety of sizes, types and

PLATE 2
(*above*) Well-designed treeshelters enhance early growth and can reduce costs of establishing woodland. (*38057*)

PLATE 3
Sycamore 16 months after planting as a 42 cm transplant on an infertile sand; no weed control. (*37584*)

PLATE 4
Sycamore 16 months after planting as a 42 cm transplant on an infertile sand; a 1.2 × 1.2 m area kept weed-free with herbicides. (*37585*)

prices. It is important that the correct specifications are selected according to species, site and application.

Transplants (bare-rooted stock)

Most planting uses a type of planting stock called a transplant. Transplants are produced by growing seedlings in a seedbed for 1 or 2 years before they are lifted and lined out in a new nursery bed where they remain for a further year or sometimes two. This practice encourages the development of a vigorous root system and a good root:shoot ratio. A plant that has spent 2 years in a seedbed followed by 1 year in a transplant bed is designated as 2+1 in nursery catalogues; if the plants were undercut after their second year, rather than transplanted, they are described as 2ul.

Table 4.1 is a guide to the minimum size of plants that should be used in most cases. British Standard 3936 defines planting stock standards for a wide range of trees.

Containerised stock

This term refers to stock grown in a pot or cellular tray containing a balanced compost. Such plants usually begin life under cover before being 'hardened off' outside. In size they can range from 12 cm seedlings in paper containers, known as Japanese paperpots, to 'heavy standards' 3 metres tall. Some species (e.g. Corsican pine) are normally produced for forest planting in paperpots.

The advantage of containerised stock is that, as their roots are not exposed during planting, they suffer little planting shock and initial survival can be higher. A disadvantage is that where the ground being planted is very different in character from the growing compost, the roots of the young tree may be reluctant to penetrate the surrounding soil. This frequently occurs on heavy clays.

Whips and standards

Larger trees are available as either bare-rooted or containerised stock and have the advantage of being easy to locate after planting. However, these plants can be very expensive and they may check or die-back after planting. Initial growth rates are usually slower than those of balanced transplants. The use of large stock should therefore usually be confined to amenity schemes where immediate visual impact is considered important.

Rooted sets and cuttings

Some species, such as poplar and willow, root easily from cuttings and on suitable sites it may be possible to establish trees by simply taking cuttings from a parent tree and inserting them into slots in moist ground. This method has the benefit of being cheap and conserves local planting stock, but offers no opportunity for improving productivity. It should also be noted that only EC approved clones of poplar will qualify for Forestry Commission grant aid. Rooted sets from selected parents are available from forest nurseries.

Plant Handling

Every year many people are bitterly disappointed when many of the trees they have planted fail to flush in spring. While there

Table 4.1 A guide to minimum sizes for transplants

Species	Minimum height (cm)	Minimum root collar diameter (mm)
Oak	20	5
Beech	20	4
Alder	30	4.5
Other broadleaves	25	6
Douglas fir	20	3
Larch	20	2.5

are many possible reasons for this, such as frost, pests and disease, in the majority of cases the trees will have been dead or dying before they were planted. Such losses can often be avoided if care is taken over the handling of plants from the time they are lifted in the nursery to the day they are planted in their final positions. Damage occurs in three main ways.

1. Root drying: even on dull, cool days a dry wind can rapidly desiccate the root system of a young tree. *Cover or bag plants during transport. Store plants in bags or cover the roots in a heeling-in trench. Use a planting bag to keep the roots moist until planted.* Old fertiliser bags are not suitable for use as tree containers as any chemical remaining is likely to scorch the young trees badly.

2. Overheating: bright sunshine on a bag, box or vehicle can create very high temperatures. *Keep plants in shade, even when in bags or other containers.*

3. Physical damage: broken shoots or roots are visible, but unseen damage from rough handling is just as important. *Do not throw plants around. Unload carefully. Do not stack on top of plants. Do not use a spade to push roots into the ground.*

Planting

Notch planting

Where the soil is free-draining there may be no need to undertake preparatory work and simple notch planting will suffice. A spade is used to cut slits in the ground in a 'T' or 'L' shape. After making the second cut the spade is used to lever open the first slit and the tree is carefully placed into the ground, making sure that its root system is not distorted. The ground is then gently firmed around the tree by treading down.

Screef planting

In this method the turf is removed with a spade before the tree is notch planted in the exposed soil. This method reduces weed competition but is not adequate where grass dominates (see 'Weed control' later).

Turf planting

This technique achieves many of the benefits of ploughing by cutting and upturning a turf (not less than 1 spade width square) into which the tree is notch planted. The planting spot is thus warmer and drier but the relief from weeds is limited and must usually be supplemented by the use of herbicides.

Beating up

The replacement of trees that fail in the first few years after planting is called beating up. It is not essential to replace every dead tree; 80 per cent survival may be acceptable provided the losses are evenly distributed across the site. However, where trees are widely spaced (greater than 2 m) or planted in mixture, it is important to maintain high stocking rates.

If losses have been severe then it is obviously sensible to try to discover the cause before investing in further planting stock. On difficult sites a change of species may be worth considering.

Stumping back

This is the practice of cutting a young tree back to near ground level soon after planting to relieve stress on roots and encourage straight growth. Once common, this technique has fallen out of favour in recent times but does have two useful applications. In the first place, damaged or poorly formed trees can be given the opportunity to produce a straight new stem. Secondly, for frost tender species, such as walnut, accelerated growth can quickly take the growing point of the plant out of reach of ground frosts.

Time of planting

The normal planting season runs from late September to early May, provided the ground is soft and the weather mild and damp, though containerised stock can be planted a little later into the summer. In the lowlands there is generally some advantage in autumn planting owing to the risk of spring drought.

Spacing

Except in the case of special systems (see Chapter 11), normal spacing at planting is around 2 metres (2500 trees per ha). Wider spacing between trees leads to poorer choice when thinning and

Table 4.2 Effects of treeshelters on growth by species

Species[a] Common name	Species[a] Scientific name	No. of experiments where present[b]	Overall growth response[c] (1) Very good	(2) Good	(3) Initial	(4) Some	(5) None	Comments
Broadleaves								
Alder, common	*Alnus glutinosa*	7			x			
Alder, Italian	*A. cordata*	2				x		
Ash, common	*Fraxinus excelsior*	3		x				few early experiments
Ash, narrow-leaved	*F. angustifolia*	3				x		
Beech	*Fagus sylvatica*	9		x				occasionally slow or poor response
Birch	*Betula pendula*	10			x			
Cherry	*Prunus avium*	4			x			rapidly grows out of shelter
Crab apple	*Malus sylvestris*	3		x				
Eucalyptus	*Eucalyptus gunnii*	1					x	develop oedema on leaves
Hawthorn	*Crataegus monogyna*	5	x					
Holly	*Ilex aquifolium*	2		x				
Hornbeam	*Carpinus betulus*	3		x				variable, site sensitive
Horse chestnut	*Aesculus hippocastanum*	1				x		
Lime, large-leaved	*Tilia platyphyllos*	7		x				often very good response
Lime, small-leaved	*T. cordata*	1	x					
Maple, field	*Acer campestre*	5		x				variable
Maple, Norway	*A. platanoides*	2		x				variable
Oak, pedunculate	*Quercus robur*	2	x					⎧ one or two trees often fail
Oak, sessile	*Q. petraea*	many	x					⎩ to respond
Oak, holm	*Q. ilex*	1	x					
Rowan	*Sorbus aucuparia*	6			x			
Southern beech	*Nothofagus*							
Dombey's	*N. dombeyi*	3		x				variable
Roble	*N. obliqua*	3		x				⎧ very variable, often dieback
Raoul	*N. procera*	8				x		⎨ then good recovery; ⎩ site sensitive
Sweet chestnut	*Castanea sativa*	4	x					tending to rapid initial response only
Sycamore	*Acer pseudoplatanus*	8		x				
Walnut, black	*Juglans nigra*	3		x				⎧ both species very site
Walnut, common	*J. regia*	3		x				⎩ sensitive
Whitebeam	*Sorbus aria*	3				x		
Wingnut	*Pterocarya × rehderana*	3				x		
Conifers								
Douglas fir	*Pseudotsuga menziesii*	3		x				
Grand fir	*Abies grandis*	5				x		
Japanese larch	*Larix kaempferi*	5			x			
Pine	*Pinus*							
Corsican	*P. nigra* var. *maritima*	8		x				branches constricted
Bishop	*P. muricata*	5		x				site sensitive
Spruce, Norway	*Picea abies*	3		x				⎧ both very variable in their
Spruce, Sitka	*P. sitchensis*	5		x				⎩ response
Western hemlock	*Tsuga heterophylla*	8					x	significant response on only one site
Western red cedar	*Thuja plicata*	8		x				site sensitive
Yew	*Taxus baccata*	3		x				still very slow growing!

Notes for Table 4.2:

(a) Omission of a species from the list should not be interpreted as being unsuitable for growing in treeshelters; it simply has not been formally evaluated.

(b) Mostly experiments specifically comparing species' performance in treeshelters. There are many other experiments with shelters and now a considerable amount of field experience but mostly with the main forest species.

(c) Overall growth response
1. *Very good.* Species showing consistently good response to shelters, usually more than doubling rate of height growth in first 2–3 years after planting.
2. *Good.* Generally show a significant improvement in growth on most sites but not as marked as in 1.
3. *Initial.* Species which initially respond well to shelters but, because of early emergence from the top (end of first or during second year) and naturally fast growth anyway, do not sustain a large significant improvement beyond the third year.
4. *Some.* On average growth appears somewhat improved by shelters but either there is great variability or, in the experiments in question, the improvement was not statistically significant.
5. *None.* Shelters confer little advantage, or may even be detrimental.

usually poorer tree form. However, spacings up to 3 m may be appropriate when there is existing woody growth to grow up with the young trees.

Treeshelters

Treeshelters are transluscent plastic tubes placed around a tree at planting in order to assist establishment by providing a warm microclimate and offering considerable protection. The following are the most important benefits.

1. Early growth rates are usually increased dramatically.

2. The tree is less likely to be held back by a drought period.

3. Young trees are easily located.

4. Herbicides can be applied with little risk.

5. Protection is provided against animal damage.

Most species benefit from treeshelters (see Table 4.2) and some can be expected to more than double their normal height growth in the first few years after planting.

Most treeshelters are attached to wooden stakes by means of nylon ratchet clips. The stake should be at least 25 mm (1 inch) square, or stouter on stony ground.

Although they are relatively expensive it can be cheaper to use treeshelters rather than to fence when the area in question is small or irregularly shaped (see Figure 6.6). In more extensive planting schemes treeshelters may still have a role in protecting the more valuable or susceptible tree species.

Colour and size

There is no evidence to suggest that one colour of treeshelter is better than another, except when treeshelters are being used to protect underplanting where light levels are already low and pale coloured shelters may be better.

The diameter of the treeshelter is unimportant but height will be critical when protection against animals is a major consideration. Treeshelters are normally 1.2 m long as this will give protection against roe deer, the highest reaching browsing animal in most of lowland Britain. If red, sika or fallow deer are present 1.8 m shelters must be used. Where rabbits present the only risk of animal damage, 60 cm shelters are sufficient.

Maintenance

Most treeshelters are manufactured from polypropylene formulated to begin to break down after 5 years. It is important that the shelters are not removed before this time as the young trees may not be sturdy enough to support themselves. As the plastic degrades it will be necessary to clear the larger pieces of debris to prevent a litter problem.

Treeshelters are not a substitute for weeding and normal practice should be followed (see below).

Weed Control

Effects of weeds

Weeds can kill young trees by competing for light, nutrients and moisture, the latter becoming critical when the ground cover is dominated by grasses. Research into the effects of weeds has shown repeatedly that grass around the tree must be killed, using herbicide or mulch mats. It is not sufficient to cut grass – in fact this can make the situation worse by invigorating the growth of the grass.

1. Cutting is effective only for species that smother young trees without competing for moisture, such as bracken and bramble.

2. Cultivation around trees or ploughing prior to planting will give some initial relief but will require supplementary control.

3. Ground cultivation can be effective but may damage tree roots. Possible methods include hoeing, which is labour intensive but permits greater care, and inter-row cultivation using a tractor mounted scarifier.

4. Herbicides offer the most effective option but the work must be done carefully. It is tempting to spray right up to the base of the tree but a small clump of weeds of up to 10 cm diameter around the stem is not critical.

5. Mulching takes many forms but the most suitable methods involve laying a polythene sheet of at least 1 metre square around the tree. This should be secured all round, using stones or turfs, to try to prevent entry by voles which can damage the stem. The main advantage of mulch mats is that they can be laid in winter before the weeds start growing and when other work loads are light.

In all cases control should be maintained for 3 years and concentrated on an area of about 1 square metre around each tree. Weeding should begin early in the season when grass starts to grow, as soil moisture deficits can develop quickly. Wherever possible, weed control should start in the year before planting.

Woody weeds

Regrowth from woody species such as hazel and willow can be very competitive. This is best controlled by cutting back and spraying the new shoots with glyphosate during the following spring.

Detailed advice on herbicides and application methods can be found in Forestry Commission Bulletin 80 *Farm woodland planning* and in the forthcoming Forestry Commission Bulletin which is in preparation for early 1989 to replace the now out-of-print FC Booklet 51 *The use of herbicides in the forest*.

Cleaning

When woody weeds grow back repeatedly and chemical control is not feasible, cleaning operations must be undertaken until the crop is free from competition. This may be ten or more years after planting.

This work is laborious and can often be avoided if effective control is carried out in the first few years of the woodland's life. Nevertheless, it may be possible to accept some natural regeneration as a component of the woodland if the species is suitable (perhaps birch, alder or pine), particularly where some of the planted trees have failed.

Fertilisers

It is very unlikely that nutrients will be a limiting factor for tree growth on farm soils and neither will luxury treatments of extra fertiliser reap realistic benefits. This is particularly true of nitrogenous fertiliser which can even have a deleterious effect. There are, however, a few cases in which site deficiencies may arise.

1. Chalk downland (nitrogen and/or potassium)

2. Heathland, acid peaty soil (phosphorus)

3. Restored sites (nitrogen)

4. Old productive coppice (phosphorus)

Different tree species vary in their response to the addition of fertilisers; ash and sycamore, for example, being fairly responsive to high nutrient levels whereas other species, such as oak, show little reaction.

Drainage

Trees are generally more tolerant of wet conditions than agricultural crops and will grow on land that would become severely poached if grazed. However, if waterlogging is severe then two options are available. First, the species to be planted may be selected from the range of trees at home in wet soils, such as poplar, willow and alder (see Chapter 2). Second, the land could be drained.

In woodlands there is no need to maintain a level ground surface after drainage, so open drains, rather than field tiles or pipes, are likely to be used. Such a system is cheaper to establish and easier to maintain, particularly as it will not be readily invaded by tree roots.

The detailed design of the system will depend on the shape of the wet area and the lie of the land, but reasonable guidelines are to aim for a 3 per cent fall (i.e. approx. 1 ft fall for every 30 ft run) and a spacing of between 20 and 50 m (60 to 160 ft). Once the trees are over around 5 years old they themselves can make a substantial contribution to the maintenance of dry, aerobic conditions provided growth rates have been satisfactory.

Further Reading

Forestry Commission publications

BULLETINS
14   *Forestry practice.*

62   *Silviculture of broadleaved woodland.*
80   *Farm woodland planning.*

HANDBOOK
2   *Trees and weeds.*

MISCELLANEOUS
Practical work in farm woods. ADAS Leaflets P3017–P3024. MAFF/FC.

Other publications

BECKETT, K. AND BECKETT, G. (1979). *Planting native trees and shrubs.* Jarrold, London.
BLYTH, J., EVANS, J., MUTCH, W.E.S. AND SIDWELL, C. (1987). *Farm woodland management.* Farming Press, Ipswich.

5 Maintaining and harvesting the woodland

Once trees have grown into the thicket phase, woodland is considered established. No matter what the management objective these trees will continue to grow and if kept will produce timber. This chapter is concerned with those operations and activities leading to the production of timber for sale or use on the farm.

Felling Regulations

With few exceptions a felling licence is required in the United Kingdom before felling of trees can take place. The licensing authority is the Forestry Commission. This does not apply in Northern Ireland where felling licences are not required. Information about felling regulations is available in the unpriced Forestry Commission booklet *Control of tree felling*.

Timber from Farms

Timber markets usually handle relatively large quantities of the commodity. This makes for some difficulty in disposing of timber from small farm woodlands. Timber merchants who deal in standing or round timber require sufficient timber value to justify the cost of moving their harvesting equipment and to cover the cost of haulage of round timber before committing themselves to buying. Inevitably this means that a successful sale from a small wood is more likely if the individual trees are of the highest quality. Remember that it is possible to grow up to 100 or so top quality final crop trees per hectare (around 50 per acre). At the other extreme, the work in preparing marketable produce will be much greater per unit volume for smaller trees and lower grades of produce. This is a vital point for managers of farm woodland and the advice in this chapter is based on the premise that every attempt will be made to produce the highest quality of relatively large dimension timber.

There is a second reason for the need to produce high value timber. Quality timber can be felled and sold in small quantities, even lorry loads. Such small-scale harvesting often carries with it the benefits of gradual regeneration, maintenance of game and wildlife cover, visual amenity and landscaping continuity. In other words, production of the highest quality trees will allow flexibility of management to meet several other objectives.

Pruning

In untouched woodland the competition for light inevitably means that leaves on lower branches are suppressed and the branches die. In the course of time, aided by wind, insects and rotting fungi, branches are shed and the stem of the tree becomes relatively clean. The stumps of branches are embedded by outward growth of the tree stem. All the timber grown outside the embedded knot is called clear and the more clear timber in the final log, the higher the timber quality. The earlier pruning is done the more clear timber will be produced. However, if too many live branches are removed the growth rate of the whole tree is reduced because the leaf area is diminished. Good pruning concentrates on removing dead branches and those contributing little to tree growth at the very bottom of the live crown.

There are particular points to note about pruning of live branches. The swelling of the trunk at the base of branches should not be cut. A clean cut is required just beyond this point (Figure 5.1). Large branches may split if a top cut only is used and this can lead to a jagged branch stump or at worst a tear down the tree stem. Clean, neat pruning of branches close to the stem reduces the chance of infection.

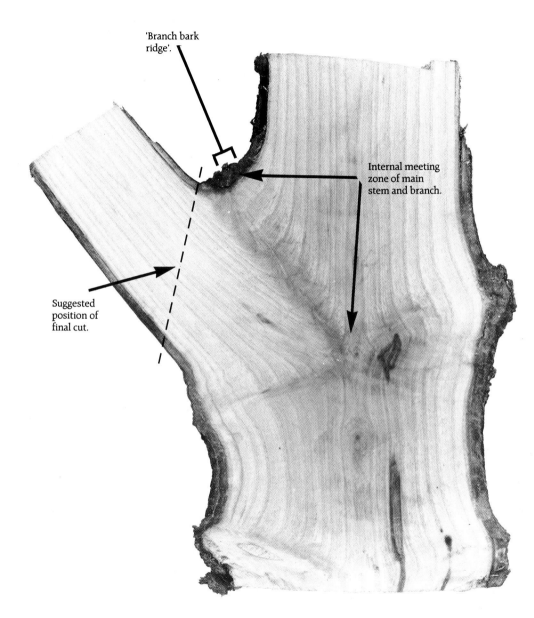

'Branch bark ridge'.

Internal meeting zone of main stem and branch.

Suggested position of final cut.

FIGURE 5.1
Section of sycamore stem showing the relationship between branch base anatomy and a recommended pruning position. (*A10558*)

39

Some species can grow small shoots, called epicormics, out of otherwise clean stems. This can happen after heavy thinning when direct sunlight can reach the stem. If they remain small these branches produce pin-sized knots in sawn timber or veneers, very often in clusters. While removal of epicormics is usually not worthwhile, their presence is generally considered a minor degrading feature. However, there is sometimes a premium on oak veneer with this marking when it is known as a cat's paw feature.

Pruning is a costly exercise and is rarely practised extensively in forestry in Britain. In farm woodlands it should be confined to those trees which are to be part of the final crop and a record of pruning is necessary if any premium is to be obtained for the timber. As with thinning, 'a little and often' is also a good maxim for pruning.

Thinning

By deliberately reducing the numbers of trees during the life of a woodland, managers attempt to concentrate timber production on a few good quality trees. These trees are selected on the basis of their form, that is their straightness and branching habit. Although the quality of trees removed is lower and therefore fetches a lower price than the final crop, it does produce a useful intermediate return.

The timing of the first thinning and interval between thinnings is determined by a number of factors. The rate of growth of the trees is important. Fast growing larch may need to be thinned as early as 10 years after planting and thereafter every 3 years; however, most conifers are normally thinned after 20 years of age on a cycle of 5 years. Slow growing hardwoods may be thinned later and subsequently at much longer intervals. Table 5.1 gives details of the age for first thinning by species.

Advice on how to thin individual crops, what volumes to remove and how these are related to the yield class, is contained in Forestry Commission Field Book 2 *Thinning control* and in Forestry Commission Booklet 48 *Yield tables for forest management*. In forestry, the operation of thinning is usually carried out over a relatively large area at any one time in order to maximise net income. The timing of such an operation often involves compromise between the urgency for crop improvement and the need to maximise income from the thinning operation as a whole. For a small farm wood it might be possible to go to the other extreme with only a few trees being removed each year to be used on the farm. A system based on relatively frequent light thinning has the advantage that a very even rate of individual tree growth might be maintained, which would add to the quality of the timber produced. One of the disadvantages of long intervals between thinning is that competition between trees is allowed to persist for too long and individual tree annual increment is reduced only to increase again after thinning. Such an uneven growth pattern may reduce the quality of the wood.

The operation of selecting the trees to be removed in thinning requires some skill in recognising the trees which should be kept and the effect of removing those competing with them above and below ground. The actual felling and extraction operation also requires skill. Felled trees can become caught up in the crowns of the remaining crop, leading to potentially lethal situations for operators of saws. Extraction must be done with care to avoid rubbing bark from the trees to be left. Such damage can lead to ingress of rot and the subsequent down-grading of the wood.

On old woodland sites hardwoods frequently grow in dense thickets in their early years, due to thick natural regeneration. Before selection of individual stems is possible, the large numbers must be reduced. This can be achieved in extensive areas of dense natural regeneration by cutting swathes through the crop using a tractor and swipe.

Single planted trees require more care because there are fewer from which to select a final crop. In this case it may be worthwhile pruning branches to improve the form of some individuals.

Thinning of a wood with more than one tree species has to be more carefully planned because the different species of tree will grow at different rates and the slower grown species may be lost unless specially favoured.

Action is required for the removal of fast growing species which produce coarsely branched or crooked stems as may occur where conifers were planted to nurse hardwoods. If left too long, rapidly growing conifers may overtop the preferred hardwoods which will begin to die out. Well timed thinning out of conifers prevents this as well as providing useful intermediate produce.

Some trees can tolerate being overtopped and these can form an understorey in the woodland. Understorey trees must be shade tolerant and be able to grow satisfactorily in less than full light. Their function may be twofold. They may be grown with a

PLATE 5
A well-developed understorey in a heavily thinned mixed woodland. Timber trees have been pruned.

PLATE 6
Quality oak timber from a small felling in a farm woodland. The branchwood is sold for pulp and firewood.

Table 5.1 Standard thinning ages

Species	Spacing (m)	Yield class													
		30	28	26	24	22	20	18	16	14	12	10	8	6	4
Scots pine	1.4									21	23	25	29	33	40
	2.0									22	24	27	31	35	45
	2.4									24	26	29	34	39	49
Corsican pine	1.4						18	19	20	21	23	25	28	33	
	2.0						19	20	21	22	24	27	30	36	
	2.4						20	22	23	25	27	30	34	41	
Lodgepole pine	1.5									19	21	23	26	31	40
	2.0									20	22	25	28	34	44
	2.4									21	24	27	31	38	48
Sitka spruce	1.7				18	18	19	20	21	22	24	26	29	33	
	2.0				18	19	20	21	22	23	25	27	30	35	
	2.4				19	20	21	22	24	25	28	30	34	40	
Norway spruce	1.5					20	21	22	23	24	26	28	31	35	
	2.0					21	22	23	25	26	29	31	35	41	
	2.4					23	24	25	27	28	31	34	39	46	
European larch	1.7										18	20	22	26	32
Japanese larch Hybrid larch	1.7									14	15	17	19	22	26
	2.0									15	16	18	20	23	27
	2.4									16	17	19	21	25	30
Douglas fir	1.7				16	17	17	18	19	21	23	25	28		
	2.0				16	17	18	19	20	22	24	27	30		
	2.4				17	18	19	20	22	24	27	30	34		
Western hemlock	1.5						19	20	21	22	24	26	28		
Western red cedar/Lawson cypress	1.5						21	22	23	24	26	28	30		
Grand fir	1.8	19	20	20	21	21	22	23	24	25					
Noble fir	1.5						22	23	25	27	29	31			
Oak	1.2												24	28	35
Beech	1.2											26	29	32	37
Sycamore/Ash/Birch	1.5										14	15	17	20	24

PLATE 7
The relatively simple, low cost tractor and trailer combinations used by many contractors are capable of high outputs. (*18078*)

PLATE 8
More sophisticated extraction machines – in this case a Scandinavian forwarder – can work in difficult terrain, and in skilled hands will do little damage to roads and tracks. (*36564*)

view to becoming the main crop later; a beech or western hemlock understorey might form such a crop which will eventually require the overstorey to be removed. Alternatively the second understorey type may be grown deliberately as a separate crop. Such trees usually grow quite slowly so will not attain large sizes. Nevertheless, species such as yew or boxwood can give small incomes at the time of final harvesting whilst earlier in the rotation they help shade the lower stems of the main crop and keep the ground clean.

Where managed successfully, mixtures help to meet other objectives such as game management and wildlife conservation.

Harvesting

The Forestry Commission insists that its chainsaw operators are trained for a minimum of two weeks before beginning work in the forest. Even then a full six months will elapse before the new chainsaw operator is working to his full capabilities. Operators of harvesting, extraction and loading equipment require even longer training to achieve full efficiency. The safety aspects of this work cannot be emphasised or restated too often. Chainsaw operators should never work alone in case of accident; help should always be on hand. The simplest way for the farmer to avoid these difficulties is to hire contractors skilled in the various operations. Nevertheless, with suitable training and equipment a farmer can do the work. Timber extraction equipment for mounting on farm tractors is available throughout the United Kingdom.

It is very unlikely that a modern timber harvester which fells and debranches trees will be used in a farm wood. Such machines require very large programmes to operate efficiently. This means that trees on farms are most likely to be felled by hand, using chainsaws. The correct blade length for size of trees is important and a properly sharpened chain increases cutting speed. Felling direction should be worked out beforehand to make felling safe and extraction as simple as possible. Extraction methods, whether logs are to be carried out on trailers or dragged out of the wood, should be worked out in advance as well as the actual routes for extraction. Places where timber can be stacked without interfering with either public roads or other farm operations are needed alongside roads accessible to hauliers' lorries. These are known as landings. Plans for landings, extraction routes, and felling directions need to be worked out

before timber is sold to a standing sales merchant or any felling is started.

The preferred time for felling is from autumn through the winter to spring. This is particularly true for good quality hardwoods which should not be allowed to dry out too quickly after felling. However, it is recognised that felling during the autumn may interfere with game management and shooting programmes.

Marketing

Selling trees is no different from selling anything else in an open market. A clear description of what is to be sold is needed and as many potential buyers as possible should be invited to purchase. The weakest feature of marketing timber from farms is the small quantity likely to be offered in each sale. Co-operative marketing is a recognised way of overcoming this difficulty and there are several co-operative organisations in different parts of the country to carry out such marketing. A buyer will require to know:

1. the species of trees or logs for sale;

2. the number and sizes, i.e. length and top diameter of cut logs or the breast height of standing trees measured at 1.3 m above ground level;

3. the approximate total volume or weight;

4. accessibility of the timber from suitable lorry extraction routes; and

5. when the timber will be available – i.e. starting date and finishing date for the contract.

The seller requires to make decisions on whether or not to sell the trees standing. The advantages in selling standing are simpler management and no requirements for equipment.

The disadvantages of selling at roadside are that all the difficulties in harvesting and extraction fall to the farmer, although these may be reduced by hiring a contractor. Farmers may go all the way and convert and deliver timber to customers. This is unlikely to be the case with sawnwood, but is quite practicable for pulpwood, stakes and firewood. Information on potential buyers and contractors is required in preparing to sell timber and some background knowledge of current timber prices is also helpful. Relevant information is available in the companion publication Forestry Commission Bulletin 80 *Farm woodland planning*.

Further Reading

Forestry Commission publications

BULLETINS
14   *Forestry practice.*
80   *Farm woodland planning.*

BOOKLET
48   *Yield models for forest management.*

FIELD BOOK
2   *Thinning control.*

ARBORICULTURE RESEARCH NOTE
48/83/PATH   *A definition of the best pruning position.*

MISCELLANEOUS
Control of tree felling.
Forest Industry Safety Guides (see FC Catalogue of Publications for current list).

Practical work in farm woods. ADAS Leaflets P3017–P3024. MAFF/FC.

Other publications

HART, C.E. (1986). *Private woodlands – a guide to British timber prices and forestry costings.* C.E. Hart, Coleford, Glos.
NILSSON, M. (1982). *The farm tractor in the forest.* The National Board of Forestry, Sweden. (Obtainable from FC Publications Section.)

6 Protection against animals and management for game

The plantation, as it grows, will create a variety of habitats which provide food and shelter for animals. Many of these, including some game species, can inflict damage to trees causing conflict between different management objectives. It is best to consider the likely risk of damage and possible damage prevention measures at the planning stage before planting.

Mammal pests

Reduction of damage by animals is achieved by protecting the trees with a barrier, by controlling the numbers of animals or by reducing the risk of damage. One or more of these protection measures may be needed and will form part of the overall woodland management plan. It should be remembered that usually an animal only becomes a pest in particular circumstances. For example, the grey squirrel is undoubtedly a pest in some broadleaved woodlands, but in many parks it is not a pest and its presence is a source of pleasure to large numbers of people.

Voles, rabbits, hares, squirrels and most species of deer can inflict serious damage to trees. All of these animals except hares strip bark from trees and it can be difficult to identify the culprit.

Sometimes it may be possible to predict the likelihood of damage occurring and this will be easier if there is some knowledge available on the population status (is the population stable, increasing or decreasing?); suitability of the habitat to support the population and the occurrence of damage on similar areas in the locality now or in the past. It is important that any attempts to identify the cause of damage are done when the damage is fresh. Many of the diagnostic signs may have disappeared on old damage and, as a result, the wrong conclusion may be drawn. Also the conditions prevailing at the time of the damage may, at a later stage, have changed.

Damage

Browsing

Browsing is the removal of leaves, buds and shoots from the tree. Browsing damage is often particularly severe when there is a blanket of snow and the trees are the only green vegetation visible above the snow. Browsing rarely kills the tree and even when damage is repeated the trees often recover, but multiple stems may result if the leading shoot has been damaged. The removal of side shoots is usually considered to be less damaging than the removal of the leading shoot. Browsing may suppress height growth sufficiently to extend the costly establishment period of the tree crop.

IDENTIFICATION OF BROWSING DAMAGE
Bank voles will climb both small and large trees, particularly pine, and eat the buds.

Rabbits will remove shoots up to a height of about 50 cm and leave a sharp angled cut on the end of the stem and branches (Figure 6.1). All of the removed buds and shoots are consumed.

Hares will bite off the shoots in a similar way to rabbits but leave them lying on the ground beside the tree. A hare will frequently damage a group or row of trees.

Deer have no front teeth on the upper jaw and browse by biting into the shoot with their teeth on the lower jaw and then tearing off the shoot, leaving a ragged edge (Figure 6.2). All deer species will browse to a height of 1.1 m and fallow will browse as high as 1.8 m. Red deer will pull down and snap the higher branches of broadleaves and muntjac will bend a whippy tree to the ground by walking over it and, while holding it down with their chest, will browse the top shoots. Deer will browse at any time from mid-November to early spring but red deer browsing usually occurs during May and early June.

PLATE 9
(*far left*) Bark stripping of ash by sheep.
PLATE 10
(*left*) Bark stripping of beech by grey squirrel.
(*37274*)

PLATE 11
(*below*) A game covert which will produce
valuable timber if properly managed.

Clean cut

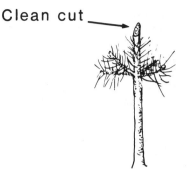

FIGURE 6.1
Rabbit browsing damage.

Sheep will browse trees and the result is similar to deer damage.

Bark stripping

Bark stripping is the removal of the bark and underlying tissues from the main stem and branches with the incisor teeth. This is the most serious form of damage because it occurs later in the rotation. It can degrade timber quality because rotting and staining organisms may attack through the wound. Abnormal growth is also formed as the wound calluses over. This causes a weakness in the timber structure and wind-snap may occur as a result. The complete removal of bark from around the main stem (girdling) will kill the tree but this is only usually found on a small proportion of damaged trees.

The damaging animal species can often be identified by the size and configuration of the teeth marks left on and around the edge of the wound.

IDENTIFICATION OF BARK STRIPPING DAMAGE

Bank voles occasionally climb trees and remove the thin bark from the main stem and branches. The bark is generally removed in irregularly shaped strips 5–10 mm wide and the incisor marks are 1 mm wide and in pairs (Figure 6.3).

Field voles will strip the bark from the roots and lower stem up to the height of the surrounding vegetation of young conifer and broadleaved trees. Small trees are frequently girdled and trees with a stem diameter of less than 30 mm are sometimes felled when they are gnawed through. Incisor marks are the same as for the bank vole. Field vole damage can be severe where sheet mulches are used for weed control as these provide protection from predators. Damage can occur at any time of year but is most likely when animal numbers are high and their main food, green grass, is scarce as in late winter and in early spring

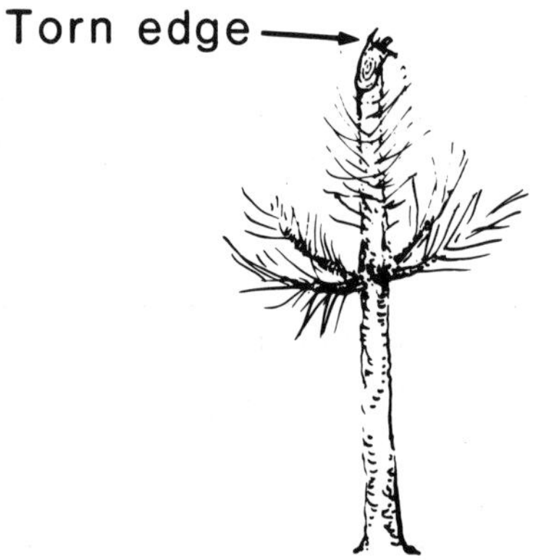

Torn edge

FIGURE 6.2
Deer browsing damage.

Bark removed

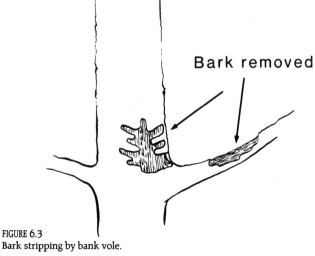

FIGURE 6.3
Bark stripping by bank vole.

when the first flush of grass has been delayed by cold weather. Damage is often difficult to detect below the level of vegetation or snow and a group of dead trees may be the first sign. By this time it is too late for remedial action. The field vole is a common resident of rough grassland and is likely to be a particular threat to farm woods where trees have been planted on grassland. In these situations conditions may quickly develop that will favour rapid breeding.

Rabbits will strip bark from the root spurs and lower stem up to a height of 50 cm of most tree species of most ages. Thin barked trees, such as beech and ash, are particularly vulnerable. Damage occurs during winter and early spring and especially during periods of prolonged snow cover. Deep snow around trees will enable rabbits to strip bark further up the stem than normal. Incisor marks are often diagonally across the stem, 3–4 mm wide and in pairs but, because each incisor is deeply grooved, close inspection of the damage will reveal the presence of four parallel lines. Rabbit damage can be confused with grey squirrel damage if the time of year the damage occurred is unknown. The location of harbourage and burrow systems and status of the population on farms will be well known to most farmers. Rabbits are potentially more damaging on farmland close to wooded edges with established populations nearby, than in forests where bark stripping is rarely a serious problem.

Grey squirrels strip bark during May, June and July from the main stem of 10–40 year old trees. After 40 years the bark on the main stem of most tree species is too thick to remove and stripping is confined to the live branches in the crown, which is less harmful. Incisor marks are 1.5 mm wide, in pairs, and normally run parallel along the stem and branches. Most broadleaved and conifer species may be attacked, but sycamore and beech are consistently the most severely damaged broadleaves and Scots and Corsican pine are the most frequently attacked conifers. Oak, sweet chestnut, ash and birch are less vulnerable and all other species are only very occasionally damaged. The incidence and extent of damage are high when squirrel numbers are high and when there is a large proportion of juveniles in the population.

Red, sika and fallow deer strip bark, using the incisor in the lower jaw. They bite into the bark and then pull the bark upwards leaving vertical teeth marks at the base of the wound. It is possible to distinguish the species responsible by the width and height of these teeth marks (see Table 6.1) but there is some variability. Thicket and early pole stage trees of both conifers and broadleaves are attacked. Norway spruce, lodgepole pine, poplar, aspen, willows, ash and elm may all be severely damaged. Brashing the trees allows deer easy access into the wood and increases the risk of damage. Stripping occurs from January into early spring and especially during periods of snow. Farm woods are particularly vulnerable to damage at this time not only from deer but also from sheep, cows and horses if these are allowed to move into the woods for shelter.

Pith removal

Pith removal is exclusively a grey squirrel activity. When the tree is in full leaf squirrels remove the top from green shoots of ash, sweet chestnut and walnut and eat the exposed pith. Subsequently the shoot breaks and the leaves turn brown but remain attached to the branch (Figure 6.4). This damage occurs principally on single mature trees although it can be found on a tree as young as 15 years. A mature tree with many damaged shoots appears devastated but the damage has no long-term effect and it is unusual for the same tree to be damaged in consecutive years.

Fraying

Fraying is the action of male deer rubbing their antlers on young trees to clean them of velvet or mark territory as a prelude to the

Table 6.1 Deer incisor mark widths

Deer	Width of teeth mark (mm)	Maximum height of damage (m)
Red	9.5	1.7
Fallow and sika	6.4	1.1

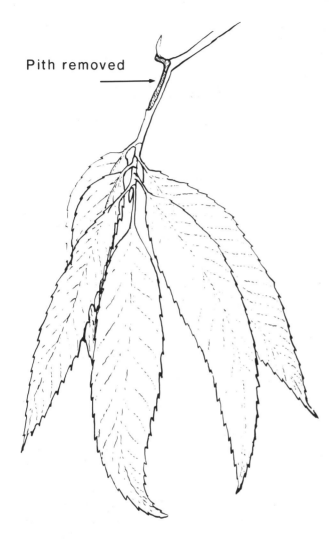

Pith removed

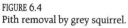
FIGURE 6.4
Pith removal by grey squirrel.

September. Only relatively few trees are damaged in this way and it is most likely that on farms they will be concentrated around the edge of the wood. Fraying is not usually of any economic significance.

Damage Control

Three methods of reducing damage are: barriers, control of animal numbers and habitat management.

Barriers

Trees may be protected by surrounding them with physical or chemical barriers, either in groups with fencing or individually with guards or repellants.

FENCING
Fencing is an effective but expensive technique. However, costs can be minimised in a number of ways. Spring steel wire should be used in preference to mild steel wire and it is most profitably used to support wire netting (see Figure 6.5). There is a wide range of hexagonal and woven or welded wire mesh nets available. This allows an overall reduction in costs of materials and labour of at least 30 per cent over mild steel fencing. When preparing the specification, account must be taken of the ability of the animals to scale, burrow or just force their way through a fence, the length of time the fence is required and the money available. It may be possible to modify an existing and well-maintained farm fence around a part or all of the farm wood. For example, 31 mm mesh netting could be added to a stock fence to make it rabbit-proof. The effectiveness of electric fencing as a barrier against wild animals is being investigated. The main difficulty with electric fencing is the high cost of maintenance and inspection, but where this is not a problem this form of barrier may be useful. The cost per hectare of fencing decreases as the area enclosed increases. The choice between fencing and individual tree guards is governed by the area to be protected and the number of trees per hectare planted. Individual tree protection is normally cheaper than fencing on areas less than 2–5 ha (Figure 6.6).

TREE GUARDS
Tree guards are made in a wide range of shapes, sizes and

rut. As a result, the bark often hangs down in tattered strips from the stem and branches. Branches are also broken and hang down. The main fraying period for roe deer is from March to August and for the other species from mid-July to mid-

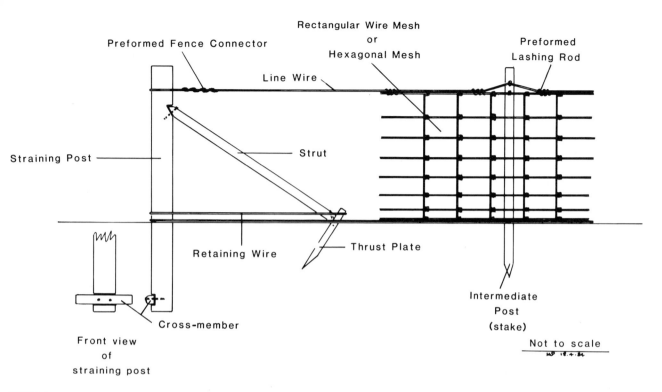

Straining Post

Preformed Fence Connector

Rectangular Wire Mesh
or
Hexagonal Mesh

Preformed
Lashing Rod

Line Wire

Strut

Retaining Wire

Thrust Plate

Intermediate
Post
(stake)

Not to scale

Cross-member

Front view
of
straining post

FIGURE 6.5
Description of spring steel wire fence.

materials. Robust treeshelters can function as guards for about 5 years after planting and have the advantage of accelerating early growth. But for longer use, purpose-made guards are recommended. It is important that the guard does not adversely affect the growth of the tree or cause it damage (see Chapter 5).

CHEMICAL REPELLANTS

Chemical repellants have only a limited value and are best deployed as a 'fire brigade' action in response to damage. This gives time to consider if more permanent protection is necessary. Repellants are less effective than either fencing or tree guards. Their application is labour intensive, their effective life is limited and they must be re-applied annually.

Control of animal numbers

Control is best concentrated in or around vulnerable woods at a

specific time of year to prevent or at least reduce local damage to acceptable levels. Shooting, gassing (fumigation) and poisoning are the main control techniques available. These techniques are expensive in labour and materials and only have a short-term effect because rapid recolonisation usually occurs. All methods of control are regulated by law, which may specify the materials and equipment that can be used and the time and place of use. (See the further reading list at the end of this chapter.)

Habitat management

Habitat management can be used as an aid to reducing the risk of damage. This may be by selecting a less vulnerable tree species or choosing a planting site that is not immediately adjacent to favourable habitat for a damaging animal. The woodland structure can be modified to make control easier, such

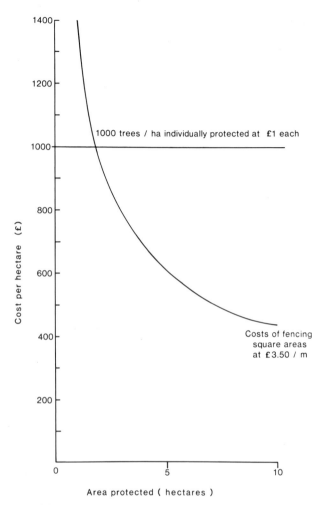

1000 trees / ha individually protected at £1 each

Costs of fencing square areas at £3.50 / m

Cost per hectare (£)

Area protected (hectares)

FIGURE 6.6
Comparative costs of protection with individual tree guards (straight line) and fencing (curve).

as providing areas of bare ground for squirrel traps or by making it less favourable to the pest species.

Specific Protection Measures

Field voles

Split plastic tube tree guards 20–30 cm tall (they must be above the height of the surrounding vegetation) without ventilation holes are placed around the base of the young tree and pushed into the soil about 5 mm. These guards need no maintenance other than an occasional check to see that they are still in place. They expand as the diameter of the stem increases and they do not have to be removed. Chemical repellants such as Aaprotect can be sprayed or painted on to the lower stem.

Effective weed control, using 1 m diameter weed-free spots, around each tree reduces the incidence and severity of damage.

Rabbits

Fencing 0.75 or 0.9 m high, using 31 mm hexagonal mesh netting with the bottom 150 mm lapped on the surface of the ground towards the rabbits and held down with pegs or turfs provides an effective rabbit-proof barrier (Figure 6.7). Netting with a 31 mm mesh can be erected on the bottom half of a deer fence or added to an existing stock fence. Tree guards 0.6 m high are available in a variety of types suitable for different applications. There is a legal obligation upon the farmer to control rabbits at any time when present. However, control to prevent damage is recommended during the period from October to mid-March. Gassing is the most effective method, although snaring, spring trapping and ferreting can be effective. Shooting is best regarded as a sport and not a protection method. Gassing involves introducing either a powdered cyanide compound which gives off hydrocyanic acid gas, or aluminium or magnesium phosphide tablets which gives off phosphine into the burrow systems. Great care must be taken when using these chemicals because they are highly toxic to humans as well as rabbits. It is therefore vitally important that only fully trained operators are allowed to carry out gassing operations.

Grey squirrels

Bark-stripping can only be prevented by controlling the grey squirrels in and around vulnerable trees during April to July each year. Spring trapping, cage trapping and warfarin poison, where allowed, are the only effective control methods.

Only approved spring traps set in some form of tunnel (Pests Act 1954) may be used. Well used natural tunnels such as drains and holes in banks make the best trap sites although artificial tunnels made from flat stones, bricks or wood can be effective. Spring traps are not baited and will kill squirrels immediately.

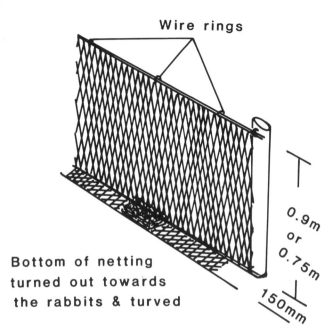

Wire rings

Bottom of netting turned out towards the rabbits & turved

0.9m or 0.75m

150mm

FIGURE 6.7
Rabbit fence and woodwork specifications.

Woodwork sizes

Rabbit	Length (m)	Top diameter (cm)
End posts	2 or 2.3	10–13
Struts	2	8–10
Stakes	1.7	5–8
Rabbit and stock		
End posts	2.3	10–13
Struts	2	8–10
Stakes	1.7	8–10

They are, therefore, useful if 'fire brigade' action is required.

Cage trapping is a relatively easy technique which relies on enticing squirrels into traps with yellow whole maize. A density of 1 trap per 2–5 ha, depending on whether they are single or multi-catch traps, is required. The traps are sited at the base of a tree, baited and left with the doors open for 4 days. This allows the squirrels to become accustomed to feeding outside the trap. Traps must be covered with polythene and sticks for camouflage and to minimise the effect of stress and exposure on a captive animal. Once the traps are set they must be visited at least once a day. Captured animals are killed humanely by running them into a sack and giving a sharp blow to the head with a stout stick. It is illegal to transport and release grey squirrels elsewhere. Cage trapping is a very labour intensive technique.

Poisoning with 0.02 per cent warfarin on wheat is allowed and is as effective as cage trapping. (It is illegal to use 0.025 per cent warfarin for grey squirrels or any of the other anti-coagulants used for rat and mouse control on the farm.) The use of warfarin is prohibited in Scotland, some specified counties of England and Wales and also wherever red squirrels are present.

The poison bait is made up by the farmer. The bait must be presented in hoppers of specified dimensions and these are sited at the base of trees at a density of 1 per 3–5 ha. To be effective the squirrels must have a constant supply of poison available. Therefore, the hoppers must be checked and topped up regularly. To avoid affecting other wildlife, any spilled poison outside the hopper must be removed and poisoning must not be extended beyond the April to July control period.

It is worth making enquiries to see if there is a Grey Squirrel Control Society operating in the area. These societies help to co-ordinate control, provide expertise and training, and in some instances bulk purchase of materials.

Deer

Fencing 1.8 or 2 m high with spring steel wires and a combination of two nets will provide a cost effective barrier. The choice of netting to use will depend upon the deer species to be excluded (Figure 6.8). The 1.8 m high tensile deer netting is suitable for fencing around farm woodland. Tree guards 75 mm in diameter and 1.2 m high will protect small transplants from roe browsing. Guards 150 mm in diameter and 1.5 m high are required for fallow, red and sika. Chemical repellants such as Aaprotect and Dendrocol 17 can be sprayed on to the trees from mid-November to reduce winter browsing damage. These repellants are phytotoxic if applied to actively growing trees and are therefore unsuitable for preventing deer browsing in May and early June.

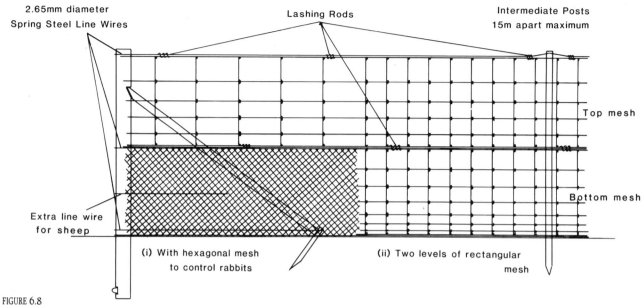

2.65mm diameter
Spring Steel Line Wires

Lashing Rods

Intermediate Posts
15m apart maximum

Top mesh

Bottom mesh

Extra line wire
for sheep

(i) With hexagonal mesh
to control rabbits

(ii) Two levels of rectangular
mesh

FIGURE 6.8
Deer fence and woodwork specifications.

Not to scale

Woodwork sizes

Red, sika or fallow deer	Length (m)	Top diameter (cm)
End posts	2.8	12–18
Struts	2.5	10–13
Stakes	2.6	8–10
Roe deer		
End posts	2.8	10–13
Struts	2.5	8–10
Stakes	2.5	5–8

Wire mesh types and patterns

Type	Pattern	
	Roe	Fallow, red & sika
Top mesh		
Hexagonal	75 mm × 900 mm × 19 gauge	
Welded	FF13	FF3 FF5 FC2 FC3
Woven		C8/80/30, C6/90/30 HT8/80/30
Bottom mesh		
Hexagonal	31 mm × 1050 mm × 18 gauge	31 mm × 1050 mm × 18 g plus two extra line wires
Welded	FF13 FF1	FF1 FC1
Woven	C7/10/15 C8/80/15	C8/80/15, C7/10/15 HT8/80/15

HT16/180/30

Shooting is the only permissible method of killing deer and this must be done humanely and within the terms of the relevant Acts (see Further Reading). Generally only rifles of specified calibre and muzzle energy can be used although under certain circumstances a shotgun may be used. Only the owner of the farm, the tenant or person authorised by them (preferably a fully trained deer control expert), may shoot deer on the farm and only in the open season (Table 6.2). The control of numbers

Table 6.2 Open seasons for deer

Red	Males	1 August to 30 April, England 1 July to 20 October, Scotland
	Females	1 November to 28/29 February, England 21 October to 15 February, Scotland
Fallow and sika	Males	1 August to 30 April, England, Scotland & Wales
	Females	1 November to 28/29 February, England & Wales 21 October to 15 February, Scotland
Roe	Males	1 April to 31 October, England & Wales 1 May to 20 October, Scotland
	Females	1 November to 28/29 February, England & Wales 21 October to 28/29 February, Scotland
Muntjac		All year round

and breeding potential can only be achieved by killing sufficient females of breeding age during the open season to balance the annual increment from reproduction. Increases in roe deer populations vary considerably in relation to habitat quality and the number of animals to be removed from populations to prevent further increase can be related to breeding performance (Figure 6.9). Between 20 and 35 per cent of roe deer populations must die or emigrate each year if populations are to remain stable.

Immigration may make overall population control difficult in small farm woods and it is probably better to concentrate on reducing damage locally.

Game Management

Management of the wildlife for sport may be an important objective and it can provide an additional source of revenue, but care must be taken to ensure that it does not conflict with damage prevention objectives by, for example, increasing population levels to a point where severe damage can be expected.

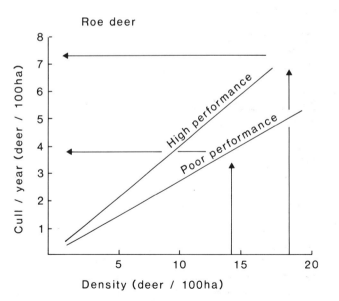

FIGURE 6.9
Performance of roe deer in relation to population density (affected by habitat quality).

Deer

Deer can provide a useful sporting asset to an estate or farm and the diversity created by a mixture of open fields and woodlands of different ages and species will improve deer habitats.

Shooting for selective control seldom means simply eliminating the sick and unhealthy, as these are usually infrequent in most populations, unless density has risen to very high levels. When the improvement of antler quality is the objective it may be valuable to leave male deer (especially the younger animals) with the most desirable size and shape of antlers. However, quantity is often the enemy of quality and if high numbers are present these must be reduced before quality will improve. There is no substitute for managing numbers in harmony with the habitat to produce the best shooting. If management is to succeed the objectives must be agreed and pursued in harmony with neighbouring land users. The forming of a deer management group is a good way to achieve this. Much useful, practical advice on the management of deer in a farm woodland context is given in Richard Prior's book *Trees and deer*.

Pheasants

The pheasant will benefit from the mix of agriculture and woodland created by farm woodlands. The birds utilise the woodland in the winter months and then move out on to the cereal fields. Farm woodland can be managed to improve the quality of the shooting. Many of the prescriptions for improving edges of woodland for wildlife (Chapter 8) will apply equally to the improvement of woodlands for pheasants. The siting and layout of the wood is crucial to the establishment of a successful shoot. It must not be draughty and hedges or scrubby edges must be provided on the windward sides. The small farm woodland with its high proportion of edge to area is particularly suitable because, although pheasants will utilise the whole wood, they are predominantly birds of the woodland edge. It also provides ample length for gun stands. Woodlands casting heavy shade are unattractive, therefore careful thinning is necessary to allow light penetration to maintain a rich herb and shrub layer. The amount of cover from ground to 1–2 m is critical if high pheasant numbers are to be maintained. Shade tolerant shrubs can be planted before the canopy closes. Managed coppice with its associated diverse and abundant flora and fauna is particularly suitable for pheasants. The larger farm wood will need some open spaces to allow the birds to fly up through the trees, as well as some rides 30–50 m in width and at least 200 m long to provide space for stands for guns.

The Instant Spinney

A major factor limiting the enthusiasm of landowners to plant woods is the long-term nature of their investment despite the grant aid they may be paid. Game coverts traditionally take 10 years or so before trees and shrubs make sufficient growth to hold pheasants and even then it is often only when protective rabbit netting is removed that the pedestrian pheasant uses such plantations to the full.

A new technique developed by the Game Conservancy in the 1970s which incorporates individual guards against rabbits, hares and, if necessary, deer, and uses a sheltering game cover crop between the tree rows, overcomes both of these problems. The crop makes it possible for the new wood to produce shooting within one year, while the individual guards avoid the need for rabbit netting. For the relatively small and long narrow woods so suitable for game, such guards are often more economic than fencing. In addition, the extra 10 or so years of shooting that are produced almost instantly provides another important financial incentive.

The planting of farm woodlands is just one of a number of possible game habitat improvements which can raise the sporting rental income and capital values of an area of ground.

Establishing hedgerows and shelterbelts, or even special game food or cover crops, to the right design and correctly sited, should offer improvements to the prospects for partridges as well as pheasants. Similarly, the creation of ponds or lakes can result in even more profitable sporting values because of the inland wildfowling opportunities they provide.

Of course, any of these options should improve the visual amenity and landscape value of the area as well as the general wildlife habitat. The main advantage of designing woodland for game management is that the sporting rent produces tangible income very quickly, and much sooner than the longer-term timber returns. Only a relatively small proportion of the potential timber growing area need be sacrificed to ensure adequate shelter and warmth for game.

Further Reading

Forestry Commission publications

LEAFLET
87 *Forest fencing.*

ARBORICULTURAL LEAFLET
10 *Individual tree protection.*

Other publications

Agricultural Act 1947
Agricultural (Scotland) Act 1968
Deer Acts 1963 and 1980 England and Wales and 1959 and 1982 Scotland
Firearms Act 1968
Grey Squirrel Warfarin Order 1973
Pests Act 1954
Spring Traps Approval Order 1957
Wildlife and Countryside Act 1981
PRIOR, R. (1983). *Trees and deer.* Batsford, London.

7 Pests, diseases and damage

This chapter deals with damage from insects, infectious diseases, extremes of weather, fire, and that due to the harmful effects of chemicals, in particular herbicides. The important subject of mammal damage (squirrels, rabbits, deer, etc.) is dealt with in Chapter 6.

Tree crops will also fail, grow unsatisfactorily, or be damaged as a result of the use of poor planting stock or through poor silviculture. Attention to the recommendations given elsewhere in this Handbook, especially on pre-planting and establishment operations, should ensure that such problems are minimised.

The following account describes, in broad terms, the types of damage that may result from the various major agents. It is important to bear in mind that farm woodland practice will differ considerably from the usual agricultural practice of dealing with pests and diseases as soon as they are detected. It is often unnecessary to take any remedial action in woodlands since trees are frequently able to tolerate what appears to be quite severe damage. Much will depend upon the purpose for which the trees are being grown. For example, the growing of Christmas trees, where a rapid return on investment is dependent on the sale of good quality trees with full foliage, requires close attention to the possibilities of insect defoliation. By contrast, a similar amount of defoliation may be of little or no consequence for trees planted for timber.

The majority of insects, other invertebrates, fungi, etc., that are associated with trees in the UK, have little or no impact on the health of those trees. A few are beneficial. Many are regarded as completely harmless and even those with the potential to cause damage are very often kept in ecological balance by a combination of natural enemies, and through interactions with food plant and climate. The conservation value of trees is discussed in Chapter 8 but it is worth mentioning here, as an example, that two of our native trees – oak and willow – support between them more than 850 species of insect and yet they rarely suffer serious damage.

Potential problems can be divided into (1) those which are likely to influence the establishment of young trees (2) those which are likely to occur at some time in the life of the crop and which could cause considerable loss of production by killing trees, spoiling the timber or by reducing growth rate.

Little attempt has been made to enable the reader to diagnose the cause of the problems: where useful accounts of the pests and diseases are readily available these are mentioned, but diagnosis is usually best left to the specialist.

Pests and Diseases

Pests

Insects and allied creatures such as mites can cause noticeable damage by eating leaves, shoots, bark or roots or by sucking out the plant's sap. In addition a few carry fungal or bacterial diseases from tree to tree.

At planting and establishment the most serious pests are those that have some part of their life cycle in older trees but which go on to feed, as adults, on newly planted trees. This means that the risk is greatest where planting is conducted on or near land on which timber has recently been felled, as this provides a breeding resource for the insect. For two major pests, *Hylobius abietis* and *Hylastes* species (see Table 7.1), some form of protection may be required. A pre-planting application of insecticide, achieved by dipping the upper part of the plant, provides protection during the vulnerable first year. Application of insecticide from ground-operated sprayers may also be considered. Advice on active ingredients and dosage rates should be sought from the Forestry Commission or ADAS if either form of treatment is contemplated.

On established trees it is unlikely that insect pests will cause problems serious enough to warrant the use of insecticides as control measures. Outbreaks are more likely to occur if there has been some form of damage or neglect that causes the tree to be stressed in some way, although some insect species, such as the oak roller moth on oak, and the pine looper moth on Scots pine,

Table 7.1 Insect pests associated with newly planted and very young trees

Tree	Insect pest	Damage	Comments
Conifers and broadleaves	Large pine weevil *Hylobius abietis*	Adult strips bark and girdles stem. Kills trees.	Breeds in conifer stumps; only a problem if conifers have been recently felled locally.
Conifers and broadleaves	Black pine beetles *Hylastes* spp.	Adult damages root collar region.	As above, but also on undersides of logs on ground.
Douglas fir	Douglas fir woolly aphid *Adelges cooleyi*	Yellowing and twisting of needles restricts growth.	Easily recognised by waxy wool and honeydew on needles.

tend to have regular natural cycles of population increase that occasionally result in defoliation.

As indicated earlier, the management of Christmas trees carries with it special problems as far as insect pests are concerned. Table 7.2 lists some of the major pests and includes suggestions as to the best time of the year to treat with insecticides. No recommendations have, however, been made regarding choice of insecticides, and the farmer should take specialist advice regarding approval for any particular use.

Diseases

Most serious infectious diseases of trees are caused by fungi, a few by bacteria. Some fungi rot the stem wood or, by destroying roots, kill the tree or lead to windblow. Others attack leaves, shoots, bark or cambium.

Some of the most serious disease problems can occur when trees are planted on old woodland sites. This is because various root pathogens can survive in the stumps of the felled trees and develop to affect the new crop. The two most important examples are honey fungus (*Armillaria* spp.) and *Fomes* root and butt rot (*Heterobasidion annosum*) (Table 7.3).

Many shoot and foliage diseases are most serious following periods of wet weather, particularly in spring. Recovery growth can often make good the damage by the midsummer. Some diseases are very damaging on vigorous trees but many only become serious if the trees are stressed in some way – for example by poor management or adverse climate.

Many serious disease problems can be avoided if the appropriate species, varieties or provenances are chosen at the outset (see Chapters 2 and 3). Only one disease, *Fomes* root and butt rot, needs and justifies routine control during the life of the crop.

Disorders

Climatic problems

The rigours of the climate can have considerable influence on the health of trees. Early or late frosts, extreme winter cold, and rapid and wide fluctuations of winter temperatures above and below freezing can kill living tissues. Snow and ice accumulating on foliage may result in branches or stems snapping under the weight, while hail may shred foliage or abrade shoots. Prolonged drought results in progressive wilting, loss of foliage and dieback. At the other extreme waterlogging, especially over long periods, can also affect tree growth by root asphyxiation resulting from lack of oxygen in the soil.

Persistent winds are one of the principal limiting factors to the growth of trees and violent storms may uproot whole trees or snap branches or stems. Lightning may kill strips of bark, odd branches, whole trees or group of trees.

While it is impossible to guard against the extreme effects of climate, knowledge of prevailing weather can help in deciding on the species, varieties or provenances that are appropriate for a given site (see Chapters 2, 3 and 4).

Table 7.2 Insect pests of Christmas trees

Tree	Insect pest	Signs and symptoms	Comments
Norway spruce	Green spruce aphid *Elatobium abietinum*	Green aphid on undersides of needles; spring or autumn attack. Needles banded yellow then turn brownish and drop off.	Inspect September onwards, treat when first seen.
	Brown spruce shoot aphid *Cinara pilicornis*	Brown/grey aphids in colonies on new shoots. May/June. Some effect on growth but the disfiguring effect on sooty moulds is more important.	Treat when colonies first seen.
	Pineapple gall woolly aphid *Adelges abietis*	New shoots distorted by gall formation.	Treat in November to February before gall formation in spring.
	Spruce bell moth *Epinotia tedella*	Larvae mine and spin together needles which turn brown and fall off.	Only a problem if near to older spruce trees. Treat in May/June.
	Conifer spinning mite *Oligonychus ununguis*	Silk spun in spring and summer is a sign of attack. Needles turn yellow then bronze.	Especially in hot, dry conditions. Treat when found, with repeats as necessary. Mites may become resistant if sprays used.
Pine	European pine sawfly *Neodiprion sertifer*	Colonial larval feeding removes old foliage.	Virox – a virus preparation very effective if used early.
	Pine shoot moth *Rhyacionia buoliana*	Damages to shoots and buds results in multiple leaders and forking. Look for resin tents associated with larval feeding in August or March.	Treat when resin tents are first seen in August or March/April. Timing is critical.

Chemical and nutritional problems

Chemicals (particularly herbicides), may kill tissues on contact or be absorbed through foliage, bark or roots to poison the tree from within to cause discoloration, growth malformations or death. Most chemical damage arises from the use of inappropriate herbicides or the misuse of appropriate ones in or near the crop. Fertilisers, insecticides, or fungicides may occasionally be responsible for similar damage.

Poor nutrition usually affects leaf colour and growth rate, and in extreme cases may result in dieback and death of the tree. However, scarcity of nutrients is seldom a problem in broad-leaved trees on lowland sites. The risk of serious damage from

Table 7.3 Two serious root diseases

Tree	Damage	Signs and symptoms	Comments
Honey fungus (*Armillaria* spp.)	Principally killing of young trees – birch, cherry, walnut, willow, Lawson cypress, pines, western red cedar.	White sheets of mycelium in the cambium of dead roots or stem base. Honey-coloured toadstools.	Disease develops by means of 'rhizomorphs' growing from old stumps. If possible, avoid use of the most susceptible species on old woodland sites.
Fomes root and butt rot (*Heterobasidion annosum*)	Killing of young conifers (most species) and butt-rotting of older ones – especially larch, spruce and western red cedar.	A chestnut brown 'bracket' (shelf-like fruit body) with white margin and underside is sometimes formed at the base of dead trees.	Especially serious on alkaline soils. Disease spreads via root contact with infected conifer stumps. It can enter new plantations by means of airborne spores. To prevent this, treat fresh stumps immediately. For information on control methods, contact the Forestry Commission's Pathology Branch Advisory Service.

site-related nutritional and other problems can be lessened and sometimes eliminated by choosing species, varieties or provenances appropriate for the site conditions and by proper site preparation and subsequent good silviculture (Chapters 2, 3 and 4).

Trees can suffer from air pollution of various sorts where concentration of pollutants are high, such as close to industrial plants releasing sulphur dioxide or fluorides. It is not clear if non-local air pollution ('acid rain') is damaging trees in Britain.

The Principal Plantation Pests, Diseases and Disorders of the Major Tree Species

Broadleaves

ALDER
No major problems but limited available evidence suggests that *Phytophthora* killing could become a problem.

ASH
The still unexplained, widespread, serious dieback of ash is not an important problem in plantations; surveys have shown it to occur principally in hedgerow trees bordering farmland and, more particularly, arable land. Forked stems may result from the feeding of ash bud moth (*Prays fraxinella*) on the leading shoot.

Ash canker, principally a bacterial, partly a fungal bark disease, degrades the timber and may render it fit only for firewood. In plantations derived from seedlings however, most trees will remain unaffected. Diseased stems should be removed in thinning.

BEECH
Pole-stage crops can be conspicuously affected by beech bark disease: heavy infestations of beech coccus scale insects render the bark liable to be killed by a fungus. Prevention is not possible, but stands often survive an attack quite well. Salvage of stems with heavy coccus infestations may be economically feasible in some cases.

PLATE 12
Fruit bodies of *Armillaria* (honey fungus) around a dead elm stump. (*27169*)

PLATE 13
Fruit bodies of the fungus *Heterobasidion annosum*, the cause of *Fomes* butt rot, on the base of a dying Scots pine. (*13137*)

CHERRY

Cherries are susceptible to a bacterial canker disease, well known to growers of fruiting cherries and plums, which is often fatal on young trees. It can be controlled with annual sprays but in timber crops these are unlikely to be economic and, unless resistant varieties become available, it would be prudent not to use cherry as too high a component of a planting scheme.

To avoid the considerable risk of silver leaf disease which results in the death of branches and sometimes of the whole tree, brashing or pruning should be done only during June, July, and August.

See also under 'Honey fungus' (Table 7.3).

The cherry blackfly (*Myzus cerasi*) forms colonies on bird cherry in spring on the new growth; it causes leaves to curl and stunting of shoots, and may result in dieback.

MAPLE (see also SYCAMORE)

No major problems but *Verticillium* wilt could be important in Norway maple plantings on agricultural land previously used for potatoes, strawberries and other crops susceptible to the disease.

NOTHOFAGUS

In severe winters the stems of some provenances of *Nothofagus* are very liable to be killed or cankered. Cold-resistant provenances should always be chosen for planting (see Chapter 3).

OAK

Many different insects feed on oak but the principal pests are the oak leaf roller moth (*Tortrix viridana*) and the winter moth (*Operophtera brumata*) that may periodically defoliate trees, sometimes leading to loss of increment; the former is occasionally associated with crown die-back.

POPLAR

Many poplars are very susceptible to a bacterial canker which ruins the timber for veneer production. Several canker-resistant cultivars with good silvicultural and timber qualities are available.

Defoliation is often caused by sawflies and leaf beetles. The large red poplar leaf beetle (*Chrysomela populi*) and the small poplar leaf beetles (*Phyllodecta* spp.) skeletonise the leaves. Serious degrade of timber for veneers may be caused by the larvae of an agromyzid fly that bore long tunnels in the stem cambium.

SWEET CHESTNUT

The only serious infectious condition of sweet chestnut in this country is the root-killing fungal disease called *Phytophthora*, or ink disease, but this is unlikely to be a problem in first rotation crops and even in long-established woodland is rarely and only very locally a limiting factor in the cultivation of the species.

SYCAMORE

The sycamore aphid (*Drepanosiphum platanoidis*) is often present throughout spring and summer on the leaves where it produces large quantities of honeydew. High populations of this aphid may adversely affect growth.

WALNUT

See under 'Honey fungus' (Table 7.3).

WILLOW

Cricket bat willow is subject to watermark disease, a bacterial infection which renders willow timber brittle and therefore unsuitable for bat making. It is kept under control by taking propagating material from disease-free parent plants and by the prompt destruction of infected trees. Legislation is in force to protect the main cricket bat willow areas of eastern England. (See further reading section at the end of this chapter.) The weevil *Cryptorhynchus lapathi* bores into the stem of *Salix* 'Americana' and *Salix viminalis* and its hybrids. It can be very damaging in osier beds as the stems die above the point of attack. See also under 'Honey fungus' (Table 7.3).

Conifers

DOUGLAS FIR

On young trees, successive generations of the Douglas fir woolly aphid (*Adelges cooleyi*) feeding in spring and early summer cause localised yellowing and twisting of needles and can severely reduce growth.

FIR

No major problems on grand fir and noble fir but because of its susceptibility to aphid attack, European silver fir is not planted on any scale in the UK.

LARCH

On European larch, to avoid both larch canker, a destructive fungal bark disease, and larch dieback, a debilitating and sometimes fatal condition brought about by foliar infestations by the aphid *Adelges laricis*, high Alpine provenances should not be planted; Carpathian provenances, such as Sudeten larch, are resistant to both conditions.

For European, Japanese and hybrid larch see *Fomes* root and butt rot (Table 7.3)

LAWSON CYPRESS

See 'Honey fungus' and *Fomes* root and butt rot (Table 7.3).

PINES

On pine transplants the grey pine needle aphid (*Schizolachnus pineti*) causes needle yellowing which precedes premature shedding of the older needles and leads to reduction of shoot and needle elongation in next season's growth. For further information see Forestry Commission Handbook 1 *Forest insects*. Defoliation of young trees, particularly Scots pine, up to thicket stage may be caused by larvae of the sawfly *Neodiprion sertifer* (see Table 7.2). Buds and shoots of thicket stage Scots pine may be damaged by the pine shoot moth (*Rhyacionia buoliana*) but control is necessary only on Christmas trees (see Table 7.2). Pole stage and later crops may be defoliated by pine looper moth (*Bupalus piniaria*) but serious damage is confined to large plantations (e.g. in excess of 100 hectares).

Scots pine suffers from a variety of shoot and needle diseases but these are only local or sporadic in occurrence.

See also under Honey fungus (Table 7.3).

In localities liable to frequent severe spring frosts, Corsican pine can be difficult to establish unless the likelihood of low temperatures at ground level is reduced by maintaining bare soil around the plants for the first few years after planting. This is usually best achieved by planting on ploughed land. In addition the further Corsican pine is planted north and west of a line from about the Wash to the New Forest, the greater the danger of severe damage from the shoot-killing fungal disease, *Brunchorstia*. In these areas it is inadvisable to plant it widely.

SPRUCE

See Table 7.2 for insect pests on Christmas tree plantings. The green spruce aphid *Elatobium abietinum* is also a serious problem on ordinary plantations of Sitka spruce.

Exposed edges of Norway spruce stands may suffer from 'top dying', a condition characterised by progressive growth reduction and ultimately by a reddening of foliage and death of the trees from the top downwards. There is an association between the onset of the problem and mild winters.

See also 'Honey fungus' and *Fomes* root and butt rot (Table 7.3).

WESTERN RED CEDAR

See 'Honey fungus' and *Fomes* root and butt rot (Table 7.3).

Fire

Fire represents a potential danger to all woodlands, the level of risk depending very much upon the stage of development of the particular woodland concerned, and its location. The risk is highest in young woodland, before canopy closure where in late winter and early spring the dead-dry remains of the previous year's grass growth may provide a substantial quantity of inflammable material. The likelihood of such ground vegetation catching alight can normally be expected to be slight in farm woodlands, but fires are possible as a result of inadequately controlled farm operations (e.g. straw burning), public carelessness or vandalism.

The following precautions are advisable.

1. Insurance of woodland against losses by fire.

2. Liaison with the local fire service to ensure that they are aware of all available water sources and access points.

3. In the case of woodland adjacent to public roads, the provision of suitable warning notices (available from forestry tool suppliers) and, if thought useful, racks of fire beaters.

Further Reading

Forestry Commission publications

BULLETIN
69 *Beech bark disease.*

HANDBOOK
1   *Forest insects.*

FOREST RECORD
119 *Pine looper moth.*

LEAFLETS
5   *Fomes annosus.*
20   *Watermark disease of cricket bat willow.*

ARBORICULTURAL LEAFLETS
2   *Honey fungus.*
8   *Phytophthora diseases of trees and shrubs.*
9   *Verticillium wilt.*

ARBORICULTURE RESEARCH NOTE
60/85/ENT   *Oak defoliation.*

MISCELLANEOUS
The recognition of hazardous trees.

Other publications

GARRETT, C.M.E. (1982). *Bacterial canker of cherry and plum.* Leaflet 592. Ministry of Agriculture, Fisheries and Food.

GIBBS, J.N. (1987). New innings for willow? Bid to stamp out 'Watermark' disease in Britain. *Forestry & British Timber* **16**(6), 16, 19.

PHILLIPS, D.H. AND BURDEKIN, D.A. (1982). *Diseases of forest and ornamental trees.* Macmillan, London. (435 pp.)

8 Managing the woodland for wildlife conservation

Introduction

Important benefits to wildlife can result from the conversion of fields to woodlands. Some will occur simply as a consequence of planting trees and will require little extra effort. However, some long-lasting benefits require continuing and active management.

Directly or indirectly all animals depend on plants for their survival and so the most important single principle in conservation is to get the management of vegetation right. This clearly requires some knowledge of the ecological requirements of the particular animal groups present or to be encouraged.

The management objectives of conservation, recreation, sympathetic landscaping, game management and timber production, can all be achieved in the same woodland. But it is wrong to expect that there will never be conflicts. For example, a landscape plan relies heavily on the location of boundaries, but special sites containing rare species or combinations of species cannot be guaranteed to have boundaries that will conform to the landscape architect's requirements.

Principles of vegetation management

The application of the important principles of maintaining continuity, variety and an element of native species within the components of special sites, edges and under the trees, is summarised in Table 8.1.

Special sites

Some areas within a woodland scheme will not be planted because they are sites of particular conservation value. Examples are rock outcrops, ponds, badger sets, old trees or bogs. Any adjacent planting should be in sympathy with the continuing value of these sites. A margin surrounding such sites should be at least equal in width to the expected height of the adjacent mature tree crop to achieve this. Open areas may require frequent cutting or clearance if they are to maintain continuity of grass and heathland species.

Some special sites may have been designated as Sites of Special Scientific Interest (SSSI) by the Nature Conservancy Council (NCC) and account must then be taken of any management provisions for these sites.

Edges

The edges of woodlands not only on the perimeter but also along rides, roads, glades and unplanted areas, are potentially the most suitable places to encourage a variety of plants and associated fauna. This potential can be realised by planting shrubs and broadleaved trees along edges with random or irregular spacings, thereby leaving some gaps for colonisation by incoming seeds. By creating an irregular pattern of scrub and tree growth along rides and roads more diverse edges will provide increased shelter and a variety of shade conditions. Shrubs that thrive on woodland edges often grow quickly and must be cut back every 4 years or so if smaller plants beneath are to grow and flower.

Under the trees

Planted areas in their early stages usually offer very good habitats for a variety of plants and animals but later in the life of a stand, especially as trees begin to close canopy, it becomes difficult to maintain these habitats. Light and soil conditions within a woodland should not remain static for too long. Light must be let in at intervals of a decade or less by thinning or felling (see Chapter 5). This allows shaded plants to flower and set seed. Sunlight also causes vigorous growth that in turn

Table 8.1 Principles of vegetation management

Special sites	Edges	Under the trees
Maintain continuity and variety of environmental conditions in vegetation along streams and in patches of other vegetation.	Maintain continuity and variety of environmental conditions along edge belts.	Maintain continuity and variety of environmental conditions under the crop.

provides abundant food and shelter for a host of insects and other animal species.

Variety

Many animals lie-up or breed in one part of a woodland and eat in another, and a great many plants and butterflies dwell in the sunlight zone along woodland edges. The woodland design should include open edges alongside a number of different tree species and ages, thereby maximising local variety in woodland vegetation. Maintaining woodland edges and unwooded places is particularly important, as the range of possible species is larger where there is more light.

Native species

The woodland flora of lowland Britain is attuned to the shade and soil under oak, ash, lime and other deciduous trees native to this country. These trees are able to support richer and more self-sustaining floras than are many of the trees imported from other parts of the world. Nevertheless, some introduced trees can play a useful part in providing conditions to establish or support the native flora. For example, some conifers, such as Norway spruce, are useful as nurses to protect native oaks from the weather and from competitors during establishment (see Chapter 4). By aiding the establishment of broadleaved trees, these conifers are indirectly helping to produce conditions in which native plants will become established.

Many trees that are not native to this country provide conditions satisfying the needs of some plants. All deciduous trees, for instance, let light reach the ground in spring and so satisfy the main requirements of early plants such as bluebell and wood anemone. Even exotic conifers will support wild plants if managed appropriately. However *Rhododendron ponti-cum* and other plants used as game cover, such as *Gaultheria shallon*, snowberry and *Mahonia*, are likely to become an invasive menace, shading out small plants without contributing anything useful to the flora as a whole.

The practices of vegetation management

The practices that influence the establishment and maintenance of a flora fall distinctly into three classes:

1. at planting (Table 8.2),

2. during crop growth (Table 8.3),

3. at final harvesting (Table 8.4).

1. At planting – continuity

Boundaries are best laid out parallel with and several metres from long established features, such as hedges, banks, or fence lines. Leaving these features outside the plantation reduces the chance of habitats becoming fragmented.

Along the edge of new plantings the planting should stop several metres away from roads and rides. This will allow marginal plants the light that they need along a continuous edge.

Existing areas of established grassland, scrub and wetland, including streamsides and ponds, have their own wild floras. For old grassland and scrub, continuity can be assured by leaving a few unplanted examples in the woodland. In the case of streamsides, planting should be kept well back from the banks.

Continuity of plant communities in space and time will be very strongly influenced by the physical and chemical effects of site preparation. Fertilisers and drainage will not be needed very much to benefit trees on rich arable land, but on poorer soils

Table 8.2 Practices of woodland management

1. At planting

Special sites	Edges	Under the trees
Continuity		
Select permanent patches of grassland, wet land, streamsides. Keep planting back from edges of these features. Plan continuous streamside belts of non-forest.	Plan permanent edge belts. Stop tree planting short of boundaries. Arrange edge belts as network.	Make permanent compartment boundaries. Set up management system with alternating light and dark phases.
Variety		
Disperse glades, patches of new forest operations through woodland.	Plan patchwork of edge treatments differing in frequency of shrub and sward cutting. Fit network of edge belts into crop mosaic.	Plant patchwork of compartments differing in size, shape, species, date of planting and felling. Fit crop mosaic into network of edge belts.
Native species		
Retain areas of vegetation formed from native species. Only plant native shrubs or wild flowers.	Plant or retain edge clumps of native shrub and sward species.	Plant or retain stands mostly of native tree species or others providing similar environmental conditions.

their use may result in an increase in the rank growth of a few large plants at the expense of smaller ones. However, drainage and fertiliser effects rarely extend more than 10 metres from the point of application on lowland soils. Herbicides and fencing may have to be considered at planting to protect trees, and these too can have far-reaching consequences. Spot applications of herbicides will be preferable to general spraying.

2. At planting – variety

The two most important aspects of variety in the planted blocks are those of block size and tree composition. Small but connected areas of broadleaved trees, arranged between larger blocks of an exotic crop, will vary the range of opportunities for many plants and animals by providing refuges and reservoirs from which re-invasion can take place. Much of this variety can be provided by a network of broadleaved deciduous planting connecting with larger broadleaved areas and 'glades', these

being unplanted areas 10–50 metres across. This 'string-of-pearls' arrangement is particularly valuable along streamsides and running through large areas of one tree crop.

A range of sizes of wooded blocks will create the best conditions for a wide variety of woodland birds. Structural variety in a wood appears to be more important than the tree species for most birds. But there is a range of bird species which are uncommon or absent from conifer woods; these include nuthatch, marsh tit, nightingale, lesser spotted woodpecker, hawfinch, spotted flycatcher, pied flycatcher, redstart, garden warbler, blackcap and wood warbler, (although the latter six are regularly found in conifer forest in Wales, either in the early growth stages, in crops older than normal commercial rotations, or where broadleaves or nestboxes are present). A few bird species are restricted to conifer woods, particularly crested tit, Scottish crossbill, common crossbill, capercaillie and siskin; goldcrest and coal tit are usually more abundant in coniferous compared to broadleaved woods.

Table 8.3 Practices of woodland management
2. During growth

Special sites	Edges	Under the trees
Continuity		
Coppice shrubs every 3–7 years in glades and most scrub. Cut most swards every 1–3 years. Remove cuttings.	Coppice edge shrubs every 3–7 years. Cut swards at 1–3 year intervals. Remove cuttings.	Light thinning in light-crowned broadleaves <10–15 years between coppicing or thinning in other broadleaves. 10% overthin at 20 years in pine, then 10% overthin at 5 year intervals. 10% overthin in other conifers, except larch, after 40 years, every <10 years.
Variety		
Cut shrubs to form patches in swards and along streams. Coppice shrubs in glades on a rotation.	Coppice shrubs on edges to form graded profile. Coppice shrubs in spaced patches. Alternate adjacent cutting dates of swards. Bare 1m² patches of soil on edges.	Separate thinning dates in adjacent compartments by c. 5 years. Extend rotation by >10 years in some stands.
Native species		
Clear brambles, leaving patches.	Clear brambles, leaving patches. Extinguish invasive exotic shrubs.	Remove conifers from mixtures with native broadleaves. Extinguish invasive exotic shrubs.

Broadleaved woods often contain more birds (species and number) than conifers, and broadleaf/conifer mixtures are even richer. Within the broadleaves, oak appears to hold higher bird densities than birch or other species. It is generally believed that native broadleaves provide better bird habitats than exotic trees, as the insects on which many songbirds feed are more abundant on native trees. Within the conifers, spruce crops appear to have higher bird densities than the pines.

Woodland edges adjacent to farmland are a valuable habitat for birds. Many birds which feed primarily on farmland, such as crow, rook, kestrel and mistle thrush, tend to nest near the edge of woods. Well developed ground vegetation alongside woodland edges appears to be beneficial to barn owl, little owl and kestrel, which feed on the abundant small mammals and large invertebrates. Pheasant and partridge may also take advantage of these areas for feeding, nesting and cover from predators.

Native species of deciduous trees can provide light and soil conditions suitable for a range of our native plants. But to do this they must be matched to the soil. The best conditions for most of our woodland plants on limey soils will be provided by planting the light-crowned ash and the lime; on other soils, heavier-crowned trees may also be used. Light-crowned trees can support a shrub layer and the variety of plants and animals associated with them, but beech will not. The carpet of spring flowers under beech may be impressive but its dense summer shade strongly inhibits shrubs, which come into leaf later than spring flowers and are shaded out.

On edges of woods, either alongside tracks or on the outer fringe, native shrubs and occasional trees will provide food, nectar and housing for many invertebrates and vertebrates.

Table 8.4 Practices of woodland management
3. At final harvesting

Special sites	Edges	Under the trees
Continuity Do not fell or extract across streams.	Extract through parts next due for edge-shrub coppicing.	Fell only in winter, in areas <2.0 hectares. Drive tractors over branch carpet. Pile branches afterwards, leaving some distributed. Leave 20–40 standards per hectare in coppice. Avoid extracting through broadleaf belts and glades.
Variety Clear fell only part way along adjacent area, except glades.	Extraction will vary edge conditions.	Separate felling years in adjacent compartments. Vary size and shape of area felled at once. Leave some trees standing individually and in clumps.
Native species Leave native trees and shrubs on adjacent edge.	Leave some native trees and shrubs on edge.	Check for influx of rare species. Keep clear felling away from areas where such species have come in. Use group felling rather than clear felling in areas where such species have come in.

Room can be made for these shrubs and trees to spring up naturally from seeds or old rootstocks by setting back the planting margin in places. But this may fail on old arable land. Here there will be few seeds in the soil and if the new wood is several hundred metres or more from its nearest neighbour, seeds may take many years to reach it in quantity. Where this is the case it may be useful to plant hawthorn (*Crataegus* spp.), blackthorn (*Prunus spinosa*), the buckthorns (*Frangula alnus* and *Rhamnus catharticus*), rowan (*Sorbus aucuparia*) or sallow (*Salix caprea*). All these, planted in small clumps spaced apart by 50 metres or so, provide caterpillar food and nectar for butterflies, or berries that attract wild birds.

Exotic species, particularly broadleaved ones from climates similar to our own, may be managed so that conditions produced by their growth can support many of our native plants. The deciduous southern beeches (*Nothofagus obliqua* and *N. procera*), like the North American red oak (*Quercus rubra*) and the European sweet chestnut (*Castanea sativa*) grow very fast on good soils and can cast a heavy summer shade after thinning. Because of this they will have to be thinned particularly heavily or coppiced frequently to maintain conditions that closely suit a wide range of native plants.

3. During growth – continuity

Under some trees, such as ash and cherry, there is generally

PLATE 14
A draughty edge. Removal of lower branches here was a mistake. An improvement could be gained by incorporating shrubs. (*E8065*)

PLATE 15
Mature mixed woodland with a well-established shrub layer at the edge.

enough light throughout the life of the trees for a variety of shrubs and plants to survive. With these species, very light thinnings will suffice to maintain conditions of light and leaf litter constant enough for the same plant species to persist. But in coppice and the denser-canopied stands of conifers or oak and beech a cycle of light and dark has to be maintained if plants are to persist. In this, the light periods need to be long enough for many plant species to re-invade from neighbouring areas or to spread from seed and rhizomes dormant in the ground. The dark periods must not be so long that the longevity of dormant plants and seeds is overrun or that the litter blanket becomes too smothering.

In broadleaved crops a heavy thinning or a coppicing at intervals of 10–15 years is often sufficient. In some conifer crops it may be impossible to maintain the right continuity as shade and litter fall are so intense. In pine crops, however, there is a distinct chance of maintaining continuity of primroses and other spring plants if the first thinning is carried out early. The lightness of pine canopies is adequate for many such plants except during the stage between canopy closure and first thinning. Reducing this period to about 10 years by doing the first thinning at 17–20 years and repeating the operation at 5–10 year intervals after that, may allow these plants to survive through a commercial rotation.

On edges, because shrub growth is fast, continuity of conditions will best be provided by cutting bushes and grass every 3–7 years and allowing them to grow up again. Grass swards intended to be maintained for their plants need to be mown at intervals of 1–3 years. This is best done with a forage harvester or some similar device that removes the grass. The cutting should be done in autumn, after October, to give the plants a chance to flower and seed during the summer. Browsing by deer cannot usually be controlled sufficiently for use as a tool in vegetation management.

4. During growth – variety

The changes that occur as newly established woodlands grow and mature provide habitat for an ever changing bird community which generally increases in both species and density. Bird species richness is highest just prior to canopy closure and heavy thinnings will encourage the recolonisation or expansion of existing plant communities. Development of ground vegetation and a secondary canopy of scrub and small trees will support more birds than single species crops. Woods can be further improved by creating glades for species such as spotted fly-catcher and redstart and leaving dead wood for woodpeckers and tree creepers.

A number of birds breed in tree holes. Where holes are lacking, nestboxes can be used very effectively; the number of hole-nesting species (great tit, blue tit, pied flycatcher) is likely to increase after provision of boxes. Small numbers of willow tit, tree creeper, coal tit and nuthatch may also use boxes for nesting. The retention of old broadleaved trees and the provision of nestboxes will encourage these important species.

The variety of features managed needs to include lying dead wood. A small proportion of dead branches from the occasional felled broadleaf tree and from large coppiced scrub can provide habitats for mosses and liverworts, as well as for some beetles and birds. The pattern of variety in clay areas may include some patches of uncut brambles as a valuable source of butterfly nectar in late summer.

5. At final harvesting – continuity

Continuity of woodland climate and soil is inevitably broken when a forest crop is clear felled, but this need not be disastrous. It does not necessarily mean that the continuity of plants is lost. After all, in the coppice system, a similar total cutting is responsible for the main period of flowering, seeding and enrichment. But clear felling, group felling and even coppicing have to be carried out with careful attention to several factors if woodland flowers are to be fully maintained.

Firstly, felling, like thinning, is best done in winter to avoid damage to growing plants. Secondly, areas felled should be kept small so that there is some change of colonisation into a fair proportion of the area before the fresh crop shades out new arrivals. Thirdly, if the crop is a native broadleaf, some branchwood needs to be left lying so as to provide a habitat for several species of beetle, as well as some specialised plants. Fourthly, if the crop is coppice-with-standards, between 20 and 40 standard trees per hectare should be left standing, together with some young, protected trees replacing large harvested timber stems. Fifthly, rutting by tractors and dragged logs should be kept to a minimum. A little disturbance of this type is actually valuable in baring ground to provide a seedbed and to stimulate germination but if more than a few per cent of the ground is exposed or compacted, the flora may alter radically as birch and other rampant invaders take over, or waterlogging extinguishes plants dependent on hitherto well-drained soil. If tractor routes are laid out over mats of cut off branches from harvested trees, rather than over wet ground, physical damage will be markedly lessened. Lastly, the final distribution of cut branches over the area can be expected to have a major effect on the smaller plants of the ground flora. As scramblers, such as bramble, will quickly cover a carpet of dead branches and shade the smaller plants beneath, it is probably best to arrange that large parts of the felled area are cleared of dead branches before replanting.

Edges of tracks, paths and rides, are particularly vulnerable to damage from tractors and dragged timber at final harvesting. Shrub growth is likely to suffer most from this, although deep rutting and compaction on and beside rides may kill smaller plants locally. Since the vegetation of these edges is best maintained in sections of about 50 metres length, the discontinuity can be minimised if extraction along the woodland edge is concentrated on stretches where vegetation is due for cutting. Indeed, the bared ground of loading and stacking places, and on disturbed track or ride surfaces, may provide sites for small annual plants to get established.

Only if rutting is very deep or the edge previously contained plants reluctant to reinvade above it, will any long-lasting problems arise. Since many plant species are restricted to woodland and ride edges, there is a risk of this happening and so it is as well to check for the presence of any restricted, and particularly sensitive, sluggish species before beginning extraction. The advice of the NCC, ADAS or the County Naturalists' Trust may be valuable.

A great deal of damage will be done to bankside and water-plant communities if trees are felled or dragged across streams. Efforts should be made to route extraction away from streams or to construct temporary bridges.

6. At final harvesting – variety

Variety in the woodland at clear felling can be brought about through separating the years of felling in adjacent blocks by a decade or more. It can also result from differences in the sizes and shapes of the felled areas. Some trees can be left standing as individuals or small clumps, and this will provide a range of shade conditions as well as bird roosts and song-posts. Clumps of unfelled trees will also provide reservoirs of plants to colonise the felled area in due course.

Because of the difference in rates of growth, native species of tree are likely to be grown for longer than exotic conifers before clear felling. This means that there will be more time in which slowly colonising plant species can make an appearance. Many slow colonisers are rare or especially sensitive to change. The boundaries of felling areas in native broadleaved crops are best planned so as to leave areas of any such rare or sensitive plants undisturbed until a special plan can be made for their maintenance. If there is advance knowledge that infrequent or sensitive plants have appeared in the stand during the rotation, then a plan of group felling is usually preferable to one of clear felling. The areas of felling can be fitted around the sites of the special plant populations and, being smaller, will have less side-effects.

Further Reading

Forestry Commission publications

BULLETINS
14   *Forestry practice.*
62   *Silviculture of broadleaved woodland.*
80   *Farm woodland planning.*

FOREST RECORD
130   *Thetford Forest management plan – a conservation review.*

LEAFLETS
84   *Guide to upland restocking practice.*
86   *Glades for deer control in upland forests.*
88   *Use of broadleaved species in upland forests.*

RESEARCH INFORMATION NOTE
126   *Enhancement of lowland forest ridesides and roadsides to benefit wild plants and butterflies.*

MISCELLANEOUS
Guidelines for the management of broadleaved woodland.
Practical work in farm woods. ADAS Leaflets P3017–P3024. MAFF/FC.

Other publications

BOLUND, L. (ed. H. Insley) (1987). *Nest boxes for the birds of Britain and Europe.* Sainsbury, Nottinghamshire.

BROOKS, A. (1987). *Woodlands – a practical conservation handbook*. British Trust for Conservation Volunteers, Wallingford.

DU FEU, C. (1983). *Nestboxes*. British Trust for Ornithology Field Guide 20. BTO, Tring.

FRENCH, D.D., JENKINS, D. AND CONROY, J.W.H. (1986). Guidelines for managing woods in Aberdeenshire for songbirds. In, *Trees and wildlife in the Scottish uplands*, ed. D. Jenkins, 129–143. Institute of Terrestrial Ecology, Huntingdon.

NATURE CONSERVANCY COUNCIL. Focus on Nature Conservation series. NCC, Peterborough.

PETERKEN, G.F. (1981). *Woodland conservation and management*. Chapman and Hall, London.

RATCLIFFE, P.R. AND PETTY, S.J. (1986). The management of commercial forests for wildlife. In, *Trees and wildlife in the Scottish uplands*, ed. D. Jenkins, 177–187. Institute of Terrestrial Ecology, Huntingdon.

SMART, N. AND ANDREWS, J. (1985). *Birds and broadleaves handbook*. Royal Society for the Protection of Birds, Sandy, Beds.

STEBBINGS, B. AND WALSH, S. (1985). *Bat boxes*. Fauna and Flora Preservation Society, London.

TRUMP, D. (1987). *Bats on the farm*. Phoenix (ADAS) No. 192, 14–16.

USHER, M.B. (1973). *Biological management and conservation*. Chapman and Hall, London.

9 Landscape design of farm woodland

Creating woodland on agricultural land constitutes a major change in the appearance of the countryside. It also gives rise to many opportunities for enhancing the landscape and this chapter gives guidance on how to achieve good design; landscape design principles are explained and practical examples are given.

Principles of Design

When deciding how best to plant woodland for maximum landscape benefit there are three basic steps to take; these are appraisal, analysis and design. A good deal of adjustment for little cost is usually possible in order to take landscape design into account in the planting scheme.

Appraisal

The first step is to make an appraisal of the landscape character of the area. It is because this will vary from place to place that standard designs are not possible. These are the factors to consider.

The shape of the land (the landform). How hilly is the area? Are the hills rounded or rugged?

Existing patterns of vegetation (remember seasonal differences can be important).

Land use patterns. Is this a landscape of hedgerow enclosure, or a predominantly open one?

The scale of the landscape. Are views enclosed (such as in a narrow valley) or are distant views important?

The most important factor will be whether the landscape is dominated by the landform or by patterns of trees and woodlands. Small woodlands have played a major part in the agricultural landscapes of the lowlands, and it is therefore relatively easy to introduce additional woodlands to the small-scale framework of hedgerows on flatter ground. But it may be more difficult in open or upland landscapes where woodlands should desirably be in scale with large landforms and reflect their shape.

Analysis

The next stage is to choose important viewpoints from where the woods will be seen (public roads, beauty spots, the farmhouse and so on). From these viewpoints obvious landscape features can be identified and noted on a suitably scaled map of the area (an OS 1:10 000 map is recommended).

Design

A number of design options can then be tried out and tested by sketches on overlays or photographs taken at the viewpoints (Figure 9.1). The most successful sketch design can then be chosen, mapped and laid out on the ground.

Design Considerations

Depending on the location of the woodland scheme, the following considerations should be taken into account during the design process.

The design of small woodlands should reflect the degree to which the landform or the hedgerow pattern dominates the landscape.

In upland landscapes small woodlands should be irregularly shaped to reflect landform and create an impression of large scale.

Where the pattern of hedgerow trees dominates, a small scale and more geometric general layout can often be adopted; in case of doubt, landform should be followed.

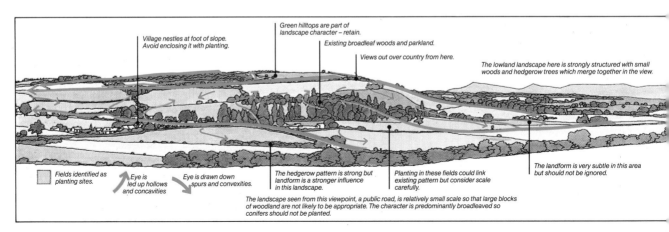

Village nestles at foot of slope.
Avoid enclosing it with planting.

Green hilltops are part of
landscape character – retain.

Existing broadleaf woods and parkland.

Views out over country from here.

The lowland landscape here is strongly structured with small
woods and hedgerow trees which merge together in the view.

Fields identified as
planting sites.

Eye is
led up hollows
and concavities

Eye is drawn down
spurs and convexities.

The hedgerow pattern is strong but
landform is a stronger influence
in this landscape.

Planting in these fields could link
existing pattern but consider scale
carefully.

The landform is very subtle in this area
but should not be ignored.

The landscape seen from this viewpoint, a public road, is relatively small scale so that large blocks
of woodland are not likely to be appropriate. The character is predominantly broadleaved so
conifers should not be planted.

FIGURE 9.1

Here is a piece of landscape in Herefordshire where the farmer wishes to enter the Farm Woodland Scheme. A number of fields are possible planting sites so the decision has to be made as to where and how much woodland is appropriate in this landscape. (*left*)

Appraisal: This sketch shows those factors which need to be taken into account during design. (*bottom left*)

Design: This sketch illustrates how the landscape could look with carefully designed woodlands. This would be tested from several other viewpoints and also accurately mapped. (*below*)

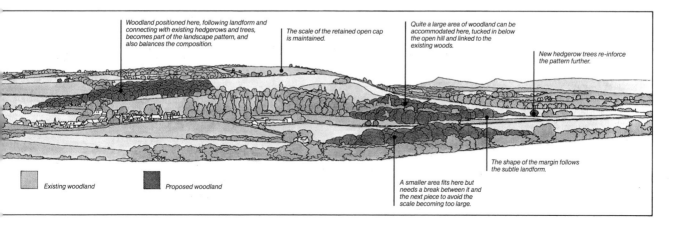

Woodland positioned here, following landform and connecting with existing hedgerows and trees, becomes part of the landscape pattern, and also balances the composition.

The scale of the retained open cap is maintained.

Quite a large area of woodland can be accommodated here, tucked in below the open hill and linked to the existing woods.

New hedgerow trees re-inforce the pattern further.

The shape of the margin follows the subtle landform.

A smaller area fits here but needs a break between it and the next piece to avoid the scale becoming too large.

Existing woodland   Proposed woodland

PLATE 16
In the western lowlands such as Herefordshire, the strong existing pattern of hedgerows, hedgerow trees and small woods makes it a relatively easy job to accommodate extra small areas of new planting.

PLATE 17
In this landscape in Powys the hedgerow pattern becomes less dominant higher up the hill and landform is a much more important factor in determining the location, shape and scale of farm woodland.

PLATE 18
This upland, open landscape in the Scottish Borders is dominated by the landform. The two small woodlands sit rather uneasily in this view.

PLATE 19
Many areas of lowland Britain, such as here in Berkshire, have lost their strong enclosure patterns of hedgerows and trees. The Farm Woodland Scheme presents an opportunity to re-create some of that enclosure and more intimate scale by careful planting.

PLATE 20
Shape, scale and position are important factors to bear in mind. These three blocks in the North York Moors are too geometric in shape, of too small a scale and are poorly located close to the hill top.

Irregular patterns should be created in the detail along woodland edges in the hedgerow dominated landscape.

Even in the lowland hedgerow landscape, geometric shapes should be avoided within the wood and especially close to skylines.

The following paragraphs provide more detail for those wishing to study design in different landscapes.

Small woodlands in the hedgerow landscape

It is important to conserve and renew the traditional agricultural landscape of fields, hedgerows, trees and small woods. The shape of small woodlands need not follow landform so critically where the hedgerow patterns are dominant in the landscape. One should consider the scale and irregularity of these patterns in relation to the landscape as a whole.

Where hedgerows are dominated by trees, the location of new woods is less critical, except that groups of fields should not be amalgamated by planting such a large wood as to intrude on the scale of the existing landscape pattern. An increased area of woodland can be more sympathetically introduced if a generally interlocking shape is adopted.

An interlocking pattern is more effective than an even scatter of clumps which appears too small-scale, especially near the skyline. Where the agricultural landscape is more open or adjoins open hill, an even more irregular shape with heavily indented margins will blend more easily with the surroundings. Limited additional planting should link such areas into a pattern of broader scale if possible.

Shelterbelts and small woods in open or upland landscapes

Although small woodlands will readily fit into an enclosed lowland landscape, they often appear too small in open or upland landscapes. Unless the area to be planted can be increased, planting should only be done where small-scale woods are appropriate. This could be close to an existing woodland or, on lower slopes, where hedgerow patterns are beginning to develop.

The shape of small woodlands and belts should vary in relation to landform, with woodland edges rising into gullies and falling on ridges. The width of woodland belts should also be irregularly varied and they should have enough breaks for the open space and woodland to interlock visually. The impression of extensive woodland that is needed in the uplands can be created by planting small woods which seem to overlap, or are sufficiently close together to give an impression of greater scale and continuity than when they are scattered.

Prominent skylines should not appear to be outlined by isolated belts unless supporting woodland extends in places down the hill face to improve scale. Belts ending abruptly on the skyline, or planted just below with a sliver of open ground in between, also appear out of scale and should be avoided. Woods should either encompass the skyline in a substantial way or be kept well clear of it.

Occasional small clumps of woodland can be planted to emphasise points of interest in the landscape or landform. They should, however, be planted sparingly in prominent positions, otherwise the eye becomes confused by small points competing for attention. Where additional clumps or spinneys are needed for game cover, they should be varied in size and spaced irregularly apart. They will also appear less intrusive if viewed against the background of a larger wood.

All these principles should also be applied to farm woodlands wherever lowland landscapes are dominated by landform rather than hedgerows.

Hedgerows and landform in the uplands

Hedgerows are found on the lower slopes of many upland valleys and where their pattern is strongest a more regular shape can be used in combination with those following landform. Woodland should be planted as an interlocking element between the open hill and the hedgerow pattern below. Wherever this pattern of trees weakens and gives way to walls, fences or declining hedges, landform also becomes visually dominant. Its influence should be reflected there in woodland shapes curving diagonally uphill in hollows and falling on ridges and spurs.

Edge treatment of small woodlands

Existing mature and semi-mature hedgerow trees in the woodland edge are of great value to both the landscape and wildlife, so they should not be prematurely felled and their crowns should be allowed space to develop.

The continuity of the hedgerow pattern can easily be lost

when adjoining woodland is felled unless some individual trees and groups are retained. Whippy, one-sided trees look unsightly so these retentions should be identified well in advance of clear felling, and space cleared around them for their crowns to develop fully.

Species layout

Because of the small scale of farm woodland, too many species in a block can produce awkward visual effects. Where woodlands are growing in a rolling landscape and can be seen from a distance, row or band mixtures should be avoided in favour of irregularly shaped blocks of single species or intimate mixtures. Generally, small scale areas of one species can be combined with large scale areas of another. Examples of this might be a planting of small drifts of broadleaves along a stream or the continuation of a hedge into a large block of conifers.

Fencing

More complicated shapes of woodland blocks are likely to involve some increase in fencing costs owing to extra lengths of fence. However, it is not necessary to follow a curved forest edge with a fence – a series of straight lengths of fencing with a little unplanted land between fence and wood should be simpler and cheaper and will, in fact, grade the habitat from open field to forest via an overgrown field area.

Treeshelters

Where treeshelters are to be used to any great extent then their impact should be considered, especially in shorter views. Brown or olive green shelters should be used in preference to white or brighter greens which contrast too strongly with vegetation, especially in winter.

Further Reading

Forestry Commission publications

BOOKLET
44   *The landscape of forests and woods.*

Other publications

DOWNING, M.F. (1977). *Landscape construction.* Spon.
LANCASTER, M. (1984). *Britain in view – colour and the landscape.* Quiller Press, London.
LOVEJOY, D. (1972). *Spons landscape handbook.* Spon.
LOVEJOY, D. (Ed.) (1983). *Spons landscape price book.* Spon.

10 Managing existing farm woodland

The Condition of Existing Woodland

Although this Handbook deals mainly with creating new woodland, many farms already have woodlands which should also be considered for management. While there is a great deal of variety in farm woodlands, several characteristics are common to most. They tend to be small in size (under 10 ha – see Table 10.1), predominantly broadleaved, at least in the lowlands, frequently have poor road access, have had little management in the recent past, have high landscape and conservation values and limited timber value.

Many farm woods are unmanaged, not because they lack timber potential or can make no contribution to farm needs, but because the owner is unaware of what can be done. The history of woodland ownership in Britain and the status of woodland in the farming of tenanted land have contributed to the situation where woodland has often been in the ownership of farmers with little experience of (or little incentive to undertake) woodland management. Because much of the accessible woodland has been cut over sometime during this century, often during wartime, the value of standing timber is often low and gives little guide to the wood's potential.

Conservation

Farm woodlands often have high conservation value. They are predominantly composed of native or naturalised broadleaved species and are often rich in wildlife. They are even more important in areas of intensive farming, where they are often the last refuge of some wildlife species. Many have existed as woodland of sorts for centuries and are classed as ancient or semi-natural. Such woodlands merit special consideration and management for their conservation value (see Chapter 8).

Landscape

Farm woodlands are a major feature of the landscape and landscape objectives should always be considered when undertaking management operations in woodland. In general, management should aim to maintain landscape features and to fit in with the character of the surrounding countryside. Each woodland should be looked at in terms of its place in the agricultural mosaic, but generally diversity in structure of the woodland and species composition should be encouraged. In woodlands of high landscape value some operations may have to be adjusted to maintain the landscape value, even if this would make them less economic, e.g. group felling may be preferred to clear felling when regenerating a woodland. The principles of good landscape design are covered in Chapter 9.

Managing Existing Woodland

If the existing woodland is well stocked with healthy trees of good form, management is relatively easy and following the guidance in Chapters 5–9 should ensure the maintenance of economic woodland capable of fulfilling many objectives. If the existing woodland is of poor quality, then there are various

Table 10.1 Proportion of total area of small woodland[1] cover by size classes from a survey of nine counties in England and Wales

Size of wood (ha)	Proportion of total area (%)	
	Range[2]	Average
Less than 0.25	11 – 51	23
0.25 – 1.0	28 – 60	40
1.01 – 5.0	15 – 47	33
5.01 – 9.9	1 – 7	3
10+	1 – 4	1

Note: [1]Woodlands other than Forestry Commission or those managed under dedicated or approved woodlands.
[2]Among counties surveyed.

management options available. Figure 10.1 gives a useful summary of these options, the choice of which depends on the condition of the woodland.

Assessment

Assessment of the present condition of a woodland is the key to showing its present value and future possibilities to meet the defined objectives. Information is needed on the size of the woodland, ease of access to and within the woodland, and the state of the tree crop. Several factors relating to the tree crop need to be assessed, particularly if timber production is a major objective. The numbers of trees and their species, size, age and quality are all important in determining the value of timber in the woodland. This information, together with the importance of the woodland for recreation, landscape and conservation, and any knowledge of previous management or statutory designation (SSSI, AONB, etc.), can be used to plan the operations needed to improve the woodland. The free leaflets *Practical work in farm woods* (Forestry Commission and ADAS) give a good practical guide to woodland assessment.

Regeneration

(a) FELLING AND REPLANTING

Felling is often the first thought when the farmer is confronted by a poor quality woodland which seems to have no potential. It is, however, unusual if a woodland cannot be improved for at least some objectives without resorting to felling. Felling and replanting is only the best course of action if there are insufficient trees with timber potential or if the woods are overmature and show little or no sign of regenerating naturally. Felling of poor quality woodland is usually an expensive, or high input, option, is rarely a panacea and can bring a different set of management problems. Following felling, weeds can reinvade a site and cause more problems than when planting bare farmland. Replanting will probably be most successful if it is undertaken immediately following felling, before weed populations build up to competitive levels. If many weeds are present when felling takes place and the site is fertile, it may be necessary to use a pre-planting herbicide application (see Chapter 4) to give the young trees a good start.

Felling and replanting need to be carefully planned if the landscape value of the woodland is to be conserved and enhanced. If a particular woodland is an important landscape feature, it may be possible to fell and replant in several stages by clear felling only part of a woodland at any time, or by group felling. In group felling, groups of trees are felled, creating openings of 0.1–0.5 hectare which are then planted or regenerated naturally. New groups are felled on a 5–10 year cycle and existing groups enlarged by thinning to allow the young trees more room. In this way a woodland can be replaced without spoiling its landscape value; however, problems often arise when attempting to regenerate very small woods by this method, as the volume of timber produced at any one time may be insufficient to attract a timber merchant and protection of newly established trees is more difficult and costly. Group felling is a good system to use if conservation is important, as it maintains structural diversity and, especially when combined with natural regeneration and coppicing, is the best way of retaining a diverse woodland flora (see Chapter 8).

(b) ENRICHMENT

This is the operation of restocking gaps in existing woodland that occur naturally or are created by group felling. It is only worth attempting to plant new trees to enrich woodland if the gap to be planted has a diameter of more than 1½ times the height of the surrounding trees. Groups of trees should be replanted in the middle of the gap, as those planted under the canopy of existing trees will not grow well. It is usual to use individual tree protection (see Chapter 4) for enrichment, as fencing will seldom be economic. Enrichment is a very intensive management system involving frequent visits to the site to ensure adequate weeding and protection of the young trees and frequent thinning around the edges of a group to allow space for the development of the new crop.

(c) NATURAL REGENERATION

Natural regeneration is a way of restocking a woodland without replanting, by using naturally occurring seedlings. Natural regeneration is often thought of as an inexpensive system but it works out more expensive than replanting if too many or too few seedlings grow. Natural regeneration can be used with either a clear felling or group felling system. In order to succeed there must be mature trees of the species to be regenerated present on the site, and viable seed must be produced (good seed years are sporadic in our major broadleaved species, usually occurring once every 3–5 years). The ground must be in a

FIGURE 10.1 Options for treating poor quality woodland

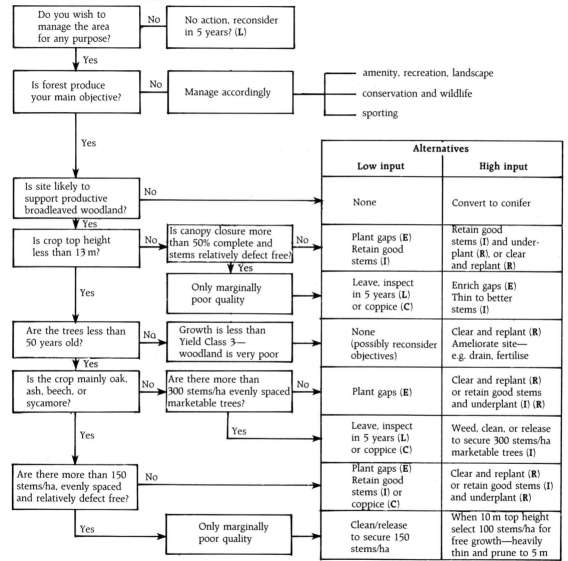

Note: **C**—coppice: Regeneration from the cut stumps of broadleaved trees, producing a large number of small-sized poles (see Chapter 11).
E—enrich: Plant extra trees to increase the stocking of utilisable species.
I—improve: Thin to better stems; clean to secure suitable crop species; prune to improve stem form.
L—leave: Positive non-intervention.
R—replace: Remove existing poor quality woodland and replant a new crop.

receptive state and the seedlings when produced must be adequately weeded and protected. The lack of protection from grazing is one of the main reasons why there is so little regeneration present in most farm woodlands, particularly in upland areas. Treeshelters (see Chapter 4) are invaluable here and can be used in an opportunistic way to cover seedlings as they are noticed.

Natural regeneration is not a dependable system for restocking a woodland, due to the factors noted above and is usually only worth considering if there is already some regeneration present on the site (or as an addition to coppicing). If high quality timber is an objective, then natural regeneration should only be attempted if the parent trees show good form and vigour. If this is not the case, then planting using nursery stock of good origin should be preferred. If restocking through natural regeneration is to be tried, then care must be taken throughout the early years to ensure adequate establishment of trees across the whole area, including enrichment of gaps by planting if necessary. Subsequently, care must be taken during the cleaning stage (see Chapter 4) to select the best stems and space them at about 2 m apart.

Coppice

Coppicing is one of the best ways of managing existing farm woodlands if the main objectives are to produce firewood and fencing stakes for use on the farm, and if low inputs of money and labour are an important consideration. It also has considerable benefits for wildlife conservation. The coppice system is described in Chapter 11.

Thinning and improvement

Even if the woodland appears unproductive and is an impenetrable thicket from the outside, it is surprising how few poor quality woodlands are entirely devoid of improvement potential. The first requisite is to inspect the woodland (by clearing tracks in it if necessary) and to assess how many acceptable stems there are – this is easiest in winter. Stems should be inspected individually and any trees of a marketable species with a good straight, defect-free stem should be marked (with paint, chalk or string). The aim is to obtain at least 100 trees per hectare of marketable potential (if the woodland is coniferous or mixed, 150 stems per hectare should be aimed for). If fewer than this

are present then a top quality final crop cannot be obtained but individual stems may still merit retention and the rest of the wood can be treated by group felling or coppicing. If there are at least 100 trees per hectare and the woodland is approximately 20–80 years old, then the woodland will usually merit thinning to concentrate future investment on these marketable stems.

If there will be little produce from normal thinning, one option is to remove all material, except the selected stems, in a single operation which can release all the final crop trees which will then require no further thinning. This is often the most profitable course since it generates the maximum volume of produce (even if the produce is low-value pulpwood or firewood) at one time. If the woodland is less than 20 years old and has fewer than 100 potential final crop trees it should be cleared and replanted or treated as coppice. If it is older than 100 years then there will usually be little response to thinning in terms of volume increment, so thinning is rarely worthwhile. If any of the 100 selected stems are of very good quality (i.e. straight and vigorous), then it may be worth pruning these to obtain a branch-free butt log of 5–6 metres in length (see Chapter 5).

Management for Recreation

The use of woodland for game is discussed in Chapter 6 and this section deals with other recreational potential. Woodlands can provide an almost unique facility, capable of absorbing large numbers of people in close proximity without seeming crowded (this partly explains the great popularity of woodland country parks). Woodlands, particularly broadleaved or mixed species, present a changing picture through the seasons, and their structural diversity which is pleasant in the landscape is also important for recreational use. Farm woodlands are perhaps ideally placed for some forms of recreation, offering great variety with open farmland and enclosed woodland in close proximity. Management with recreation as an objective offers considerable opportunities for providing a valuable resource as part of a business venture (particularly in tourist areas, near centres of population, and on the urban fringe). Once again, the first step is to assess the resource available and define objectives.

Rights of way

There may already be public use of the woodland on public

PLATE 21
Many neglected woodlands can be brought back into management without the need to resort to clear felling. Selected stems in this old coppice woodland can be favoured by thinning and grown on to produce timber.

PLATE 22
Given sufficient light in group fellings, natural regeneration can be a successful method of restocking existing woodland. (*10244*)

footpaths, bridleways or byways. The local highway authority (usually the county council) holds the definitive map of statutory rights of way for its area and this is available for public inspection. If there are rights of way the owner has a legal obligation to keep them clear. Waymarking will encourage visitors to follow the prescribed route. Waymarking of public rights of way is the responsibility of the highway authority but is often undertaken by landowners. The Countryside Commission's free leaflet *Waymarking of a public right of way* is a useful reference if marking paths is being considered.

Where there are no rights of way but public access has been allowed in the past, or is to be encouraged in the future, the farmer can waymark some paths on a permissive basis. If the farmer does not want these paths to become rights of way then he should put up a public notice stating that the path is permissive, and notify the highway authority. Permissive paths have the advantage that they can be temporarily diverted or closed during harvesting operations or for other management reasons, whereas diversion or closure of statutory rights of way is a very difficult process.

Business opportunities

If recreation in farm woodlands is looked upon as a means of supplementing income then more facilities such as car parks, picnic places and viewpoints may well be necessary and these should be designed to fit in with the other objectives of the woodland. Car parks, if correctly designed, can be used as landings or stacking areas for woodland produce (see Chapter 5). Woodland roads and tracks can be used for walking, riding or even bicycling if adequately surfaced. Opportunities exist to use the woodlands as part of an already existing recreational or tourist business, as part of a farm trail, or as a place for camping or caravanning. Some specialist activities can be specifically attracted to woodlands – horse riding circuits, off-road motor-cycling and clay pigeon shooting for example – but their impact upon the surrounding countryside must be considered and planning permission may be needed for some.

Liability

Wherever the public are encouraged into woods by provision of car parks, picnic places, etc., or there is access from a public right of way, consideration must be given to whether any trees are dangerous. There is a responsibility on the owner of woodland in places frequented by the public to assess tree health and, as far as possible, to remove obviously dangerous trees or branches. The assessment of whether a tree is dangerous or not can be difficult and is best undertaken by a professional arboriculturist, but as a general guide owners should be particularly wary of trees which are overmature (Table 10.2) or show signs of fungal attack. The free leaflet *The recognition of hazardous trees* available from the Forestry Commission is a useful aid to spotting danger signs.

Advice and grant aid

Advice and assistance with planning recreational facilities may be sought from the Countryside Commission, Tourist Boards or ADAS, and grant aid may be available from these sources or local authorities, as well as possible new initiatives under the ALURE package. Whatever facility is planned, it should be designed and constructed to a high standard and should be regularly inspected

Table 10.2 Age generally indicating significant overmaturity in broadleaved tree species

Species	Age (years)
Alder (Common)	80
Ash	120
Beech	180
Birch	60
Cherry	80
Hornbeam	200
Lime	200
Norway maple	120
Oak	250
Poplar	80
Red oak	120
Sweet chestnut	200
Sycamore	200
Willow	80

Note: Sometimes on infertile but not otherwise inhospitable sites trees may grow slowly and steadily and reach much greater ages than those indicated without the symptoms of overmaturity.

to ensure adequate maintenance. High landscaping values, particularly internal woodland landscape, should be aimed at and views out of the woodland can be created or emphasised by selective felling. Disabled visitors should not be neglected in the provision of facilities and special assistance by way of grant aid may be available for this purpose.

Further Reading

Forestry Commission publications

BULLETINS
62 *Silviculture of broadleaved woodland.*
78 *Natural regeneration of broadleaves.*
80 *Farm woodland planning.*

FOREST RECORD
113 *Free growth of oak.*

OCCASIONAL PAPERS
14 *The Gwent small woods project 1979–84.*
17 *Farming and forestry.*

MISCELLANEOUS
Practical work in farm woods. ADAS Leaflets P3017–P3024. MAFF/FC.
The recognition of hazardous trees.

ARBORICULTURE RESEARCH NOTES
35/81/SILN *Winter shelter for agricultural stock.*
64/87/SILS *Treeshelters.*

Other publications

BROOKS, A. (1987). *Woodlands – a practical conservation handbook.* British Trust for Conservation Volunteers, Wallingford.

BROWN, I.R. (1983). *Management of birch woodland in Scotland.* Countryside Commission for Scotland.

COUNTRYSIDE COMMISSION (1983). *Small woods on farms.* Countryside Commission Report CCP 143.

COUNTRYSIDE COMMISSION. *Waymarking of a public right of way.*

DOWNING, P. AND FITTON, M. (1981). *Small woods – the Dartington Study.* Conference on farm woods – management, conservation and financial resources. National Agriculture Centre, Stoneleigh, February 1981.

IRVING, J.A. (1986). *The public in your woods.* Land Decade Educational council (Packhard, Chichester).

MALCOLM, D.C., EVANS, J. AND EDWARDS, P.N. (eds.) (1982). *Broadleaves in Britain – future management and research.* Institute of Chartered Foresters, Edinburgh.

NEWBOLD, A.J. AND GOLDSMITH, F.B. (1981). *The regeneration of oak and beech.* Discussion Papers in Conservation 33. University College, London.

PETERKEN, G.F. (1981). *Woodland conservation and management.* Chapman and Hall, London.

SHAW, M.W. (1968). Factors affecting the natural regeneration of sessile oak (*Quercus petraea*) in north Wales. *Journal of Ecology* **56**, I. 565–583; II. 647–660.

SMART, N. AND ANDREWS, J. (1985). *Birds and broadleaves handbook.* Royal Society for the Protection of Birds, Sandy, Beds.

11 Other systems for growing trees on farms

The vast majority of trees in woodland on farms, and in forests, are grown in conventional high forest and coppice systems, which have been practised for centuries in the UK and the rest of Europe. There are, however, some alternative systems for growing trees which may be particularly relevant to farmers, as they integrate forestry and farming (agroforestry, woodland shelter), have relatively short rotations (Christmas trees, short rotation coppice) or can, through intensive management, produce high priced products from small areas of land (foliage, decorative timber). These systems are currently of minor importance compared with traditional high forest and coppice systems, so do not have the same well documented history and the established markets. They are therefore rather more risky investments and, in the case of some systems, they are still very much at the experimental stage in Britain and have no large scale commercial trials. Because of their experimental nature, and because (for some systems) they are unlike conventional woodland practice, they may not be eligible for grant aid under the Woodland Grant Scheme. Consequently they may not be eligible for the Farm Woodland Scheme. Nevertheless, on the right land and with the correct management, these systems can be very productive and possibly give higher financial returns than conventional woodland.

Poplar

Poplars are almost always grown in pure stands and at wide spacing. Only cultivars approved under the European Community Regulations (see below) are eligible for grant aid for timber production in the UK. Poplar cultivation is restricted to the lowlands and for the black poplar hybrids, to eastern and southern England. Successful plantations are rare in N. Ireland and Scotland.

Poplars are propagated from cuttings, usually 25 cm long, and these may be directly inserted on the growing site after it has been cultivated. Alternatively they may be grown in a nursery bed for 1–2 years to produce rooted plants. Rooted stocks are always pit planted. Survival and growth of newly planted poplars are seriously reduced by weed competition and a weed-free spot of at least 1 m diameter is essential. If cuttings are directly inserted on the site, or unrooted sets (up to 2 m tall) used, then initial cultivation and good weed control are even more important. With poplars planted at wide spacings, weeding can be with chemicals (see Chapter 4) or by ground cultivation between the rows. Ground cultivation will obviously damage surface roots but this does not reduce growth as it might with other species, and seems to be beneficial in some circumstances.

Spacings are usually wide, as competition between trees is intense. Spacings up to 8 m may be eligible for grant aid. Plantations are not usually thinned. Close spacings (2–4 m) can be used with clones of *Populus trichocarpa* and its hybrids for short rotation crops producing high volumes (150–270 m^3 per hectare) of pulpwood on a 12–15 year rotation. Markets are usually pulpwood for small material (less than 30 cm tree diameter), and veneer/packaging/pallets for large material (greater than 30 cm). To achieve packaging or veneer quality, pruning to 5–6 m is essential and may be necessary every year initially, as poplars are prone to producing side shoots.

Poplars currently eligible for grant aid in Britain under European Community Regulations are:

P. × *canescens*
P. × *euramericana* 'Eugenei'
P. × *euramericana* 'Gelrica'
P. × *euramericana* 'Heidemij'
P. × *euramericana* 'I-78'
P. × *euramericana* 'Robusta'
P. × *euramericana* 'Serotina'
P. *tacamahaca* × *trichocarpa* 32
P. *trichocarpa* 'Fritzi Pauley'
P. *trichocarpa* 'Scott Pauley'

Grant aid may be payable on planting of poplars at spacings up to 8 m.

PLATE 23
(*top*) On moist fertile sites poplar species will produce an early timber return.
PLATE 24
19-year-old hybrid poplar ready for felling.

PLATE 25
(*right*) A good, mature, mixed shelterbelt which could be improved by widening. New planting, if properly planned, will ensure the retention of shelter.

PLATE 26 'Gapping up' coppice after cutting, treeshelters being used to aid fast establishment. Some new 'maidens' are planted to maintain the overstorey of standard trees.

Christmas Trees

Christmas trees have often been suggested as an alternative crop for agricultural land and there has been a marked increase in planting in recent years. It is a crop that is not without its problems because of the cyclical nature of the market and there are growers who have lost considerable sums of money as a result. Recent calculations have shown that only a further 2700 hectares of Christmas trees will be required to achieve self-sufficiency in Britain.

In addition to the marketing risks associated with Christmas trees, there are growing risks which are dependent on climate, pests and cultural techniques. Some of the latter risks can be reduced by means of a higher input nursery type regime with a consequently lower nett return. Christmas trees can also be grown as part of a mixed crop with the intention of early removal, or as a matrix between widely spaced poplars.

The Norway spruce is the traditional Christmas tree and currently accounts for over 80 per cent of the market, but in recent years sales of pines (Scots, lodgepole and Corsican), and firs (noble and Nordmann's) have increased. These species tend to have slightly longer rotations because of their slower growth, 7–10 years rather than 5–8.

Christmas trees are usually planted at 0.9–1.2 m spacing and if a nursery system is being followed, ground preparation will be by ploughing and initial weed control by simazine. Weed control is essential for good growth and to retain live branches to the ground. Weeding is likely to be continued for the first four seasons following planting. Some growers are now shearing their trees, particularly pines (cutting the leading shoot and ends of branches), to produce a bushier tree of better shape and improve the percentage of saleable trees. Aphids and other pests are sometimes troublesome and may need to be controlled (see Chapter 7). The marketing of the trees is crucial to the profitability of the operation.

Coppice

Coppice is a crop of small dimension timber raised from shoots produced by the cut stumps of the previous timber crop. Most broadleaved species will produce coppice (beech being the only major exception) but conifers, with the exception of coast redwood (*Sequoia sempervirens*) and monkey puzzle (*Araucaria araucana*), will not. Coppicing used to be a very important woodland system and many broadleaved woodlands have been managed in this way in the past to produce small dimension products for firewood, fencing and building.

The neglect of coppicing during the last 40 or 50 years, because of poor markets for small dimension products, has led to much overgrown or stored coppice, often producing poor quality timber in poorly stocked woodlands. Resumption of coppicing is usually possible even after 60 years of neglect and, provided livestock is excluded; this is often the most successful low cost way of bringing a poor quality woodland back into management (see Chapter 10).

The produce from coppicing will depend on the species present and the rotation or interval between successive cuts. Table 11.1 gives some indication of the products and rotations likely for different species. Coppice is essentially a low input,

Table 11.1 Products and rotations for coppice

Species	Rotation (years)	No. of stools per hectare	Products
Sweet chestnut	15	800–1000	Stakes, fence palings, hop poles
Oak	30	600–800	Fuelwood, tan bark, charcoal
Other hardwoods and mixed coppices	20–25	600–1200	Fuelwood, pulpwood, turnery
Short rotations			
Mixed species	7–10	about 2000	Pea and bean sticks, hedgelaying stakes, pulpwood
Hazel	6–9	about 2000	Spars (thatching), hurdles

PLATE 27
Spring flowers under ash coppice and beech trees.

PLATE 28
Coppicing birch and hazel for bean poles.
(*37244*)

low output system capable of generating a small cash profit at each cutting, and requiring little maintenance other than an occasional 'gapping up'. Gapping up is the term used to describe the replacement of coppice stools (the term given to the cut stumps) which have died and produced a gap in the woodland.

Gapping up is usually achieved by planting but occasionally by layering stems from adjacent stools. It is usually only necessary in gaps over 10 m in diameter – if the gap is smaller the vigorous coppice regrowth from surrounding stools will prove too competitive. Coppicing is perhaps the best way of managing farm woodlands if the main objectives are to produce firewood and fencing stakes for use on the farm, and if low inputs (of money and labour) are an important consideration. For very small woodlands incapable of producing saleable quantities of saw timber, coppicing is one of the few ways of ensuring the woodlands' survival and producing a return. It is also one of the cheapest ways of regenerating a broadleaved woodland.

Coppicing can be continued indefinitely as a management system and some stumps are known to have produced vigorous coppice over many hundreds of years. Coppicing is a particularly useful form of management if conservation is an important objective. The relatively short rotations (less than 30 years) mean that the period of complete canopy cover is short, so allowing seeds of herbaceous and other ground flora to survive ready to take advantage of the light following the next felling. This, and the fact that most coppices are of native species, (apart from sweet chestnut coppice, which is very important in south-east England, particularly Kent, East and West Sussex), leads to a particularly rich ground flora. Most coppice crops are also worked in small areas at a time and this gives the woodland structural diversity and a variety of habitats able to support a wide range of wildlife (see Chapter 8).

Coppicing is an ideal system for the production of a range of small dimension products such as firewood, fencing stakes, pulpwood, charcoal and turnery poles. If, however, the main objective is to produce saw timber, coppice can be converted to high forest by singling. This is best done while the coppice regrowth is relatively young (less than 15 years) and is achieved by removing all stems except the best (straightest, most vigorous) on each stool. The stems which are grown on to form large trees are known as stored coppice. Once the singling operation is done the woodland can be treated as high forest for subsequent thinning and felling (see Chapter 5). The stems produced from stored coppice may not be of the same quality as those from maiden trees due to the greater basal sweep in the butt log and possible butt rot developing from the old stump.

The system that includes some timber sized trees (known as 'standards') within a coppice woodland is called coppice with standards. In this system the coppice forms a second canopy (understorey) underneath the standards. The standard trees can be the result of natural regeneration, stored coppice shoots or planting. The crowns of the standard trees generally occupy about 30–40 per cent of the ground area and they should not be allowed to occupy more space or they will reduce the amount of light needed to maintain healthy vigorous coppice. The most common standard tree is oak and it is traditional to have standard trees of several different ages in any one area. Some mature standards are felled at each coppicing and some new ones established (preferably by planting). Coppice with standards is even better than pure coppice for conservation as it retains all the benefits of coppice working and in addition has an overstorey of standard trees, bringing still more structural diversity. Coppice with standards is also undoubtedly one of the best systems where landscape considerations have a high priority, as the outward appearance of the woodland does not appear to change, even after each felling cycle. The internal appearance is also structurally diverse and very pleasant to look at.

Short Rotation Coppice

Coppice having a rotation of less than 10 years, and generally producing small sized material, can be regarded as short rotation coppice. It is not a new concept but experimental work has been undertaken in the UK recently to try to find out the best techniques to maximise output from these systems, in terms of dry weight production. It has been thought that production of a renewable material may be important in producing energy in the future, through burning wood chips. However, this is not yet an established market and any wood produced in this system at present would have to supply existing markets, mainly pulpwood and traditional firewood.

The growing of short rotation coppice is very like an arable farming crop, but on a cycle of perhaps 4 years, rather than 1 year. The species which have proved most successful in the UK over a range of sites and climatic conditions have been poplars and willows, though several others are under investigation.

PLATE 29
Cleft fencing material produced from sweet chestnut coppice.

PLATE 30
Short rotation coppice: 4-year-old hybrid poplar on farmland (the ranging rod is 2 metres high).

Ground preparation is most effective by cultivation, usually ploughing, and killing any vegetation before cultivation also improves yields.

Optimum spacing will vary, depending on the length of cutting cycle and species chosen. For cycles of 6–8 years producing larger sized end products, wider spacings of 1.5–3 m optimise production, while for short rotations of 2–4 years closer spacings 0.5–1 m are more appropriate. Willows are usually spaced closer than poplars. Cuttings 25–50 cm long are inserted into the cultivated ground. Weed control at the early stages of establishment is crucial and heavy weed competition in the first years will severely reduce final yields. The growth at the end of the first year is cut back to near ground level to form the coppice stool. One benefit of close spacing is that coppice regrowth will quickly shade out the soil and kill any competing weeds.

Assuming a well stocked vigorous coppice has been produced, the total production can be expected to be in the region of 10–16 tonnes dry matter per hectare per year. Pests and diseases can be a problem, particularly rust diseases on willows, and these can reduce yields (see Chapter 7). The high production rates of this system are very tempting but the techniques are still experimental, and these systems are not currently eligible for grant aid except in Northern Ireland.

Agroforestry

Agroforestry is an intimate mixture of trees with farm crops and/or animals on the same piece of land. In temperate regions it usually consists of widely spaced individual trees, groups or lines of trees in grazed or arable fields. Agroforestry systems have proved successful abroad (notably New Zealand) and are now being tested experimentally in the UK.

It is likely that in the UK trees in grazed pastures will be the most important system, though poplars with arable intercrops have been successful in England. Species choice is limited to trees with good apical dominance (trees that tend to keep a single main stem rather than splitting into several main branches low down on their trunks), capable of producing quality timber in an open situation. The main broadleaved species suitable are sycamore, ash, cherry, walnut (only in southern England, and requires pruning to shape the main stem), and poplar, while the most suitable conifers are Douglas

fir, Corsican pine and hybrid larch.

Rotations are likely to be 35–45 years, with poplar rather shorter at 20 years and walnut longer at about 60 years. The aim is to produce a saleable butt log of high quality timber of approximately 45 cm diameter, with a minimum reduction in agricultural production for the first 10–15 years. As the trees grow and the grass is progressively shaded, the timber value increases and the agricultural return decreases. Economic models have shown that the yield from agroforestry can be expected to be slightly higher than that from pure sheep grazing or dairy cattle in the lowlands, and higher than that for a woodland crop. It must be stressed, however, that these models are based upon assumptions which have not been field tested in the UK.

Only the best quality planting stock should be used as there is virtually no chance of selection through thinning. Pit planting is essential for walnut and poplar and recommended for others. Spacings are usually 5–15 m. Initial protection against grazing animals will be necessary, as even if the area is to be cut as silage or hay and not stocked with animals, rabbits and hares can do major damage. Initial protection can be either strip fencing or individual tree protection, in which case at least two stakes per tree, in addition to a treeshelter, will be needed to protect against cattle and sheep rubbing. A weed-free spot of about 1 m diameter is needed for successful establishment.

Pruning is essential to produce quality timber but should never remove more than 30 per cent of the live crown at one time. An ultimate branch-free height of 4–6 m should be aimed for. Careful choice of species and spacings should allow trees to reach maturity and be harvested over a prolonged period of time (30–80 years), helping to even out cash flow and giving a more even carrying capacity for grazing stock. Agricultural rates of fertiliser to maintain the grass sward are unlikely to make the trees grow faster (with the possible exception of ash), and very high rates may be deleterious to production of quality timber by causing distortions in tree growth. Agroforestry is not currently eligible for grant aid under the Woodland Grant Scheme or Farm Woodland Scheme.

Hedgerow Trees

Hedgerow trees are an important source of hardwood timber. They are also of great conservation and landscape value, provide a distinct land boundary and give some shelter to livestock. Most hedgerow trees are recruited by letting existing saplings within the hedge develop into mature trees. This can be achieved by leaving small sections of hedgerow uncut for 2 or 3 years, then selecting stems of suitable species to develop into timber trees. The same result can be achieved by planting new trees in, or adjacent to, an existing hedge but expensive protection is needed if stock is present. Rabbit or deer protection may still be needed in arable areas, and the use of treeshelters can be an effective method of protection in these circumstances (see Chapter 4). Hedgerow trees should be spaced at least 8 m apart, and no thinning is necessary. The value of hedgerow trees can be improved by pruning, but their value will often be less than a similar tree from woodland, because timber merchants disregard the bottom 1.5 m (5 ft) of stem in calculating volume, as this often has damage from old wounds causing rot, or metal from old fencing. Most species are suitable, particularly broad-leaved trees and especially trees such as field maple and holly which do not suffer from serious disease following wounding, and can also form part of a thick, conventionally cut hedge.

Cricket Bat Willow

One cultivar of willow, *Salix alba* cultivar 'Coerulea', is grown specifically for the manufacture of cricket bats. Cricket bat willow can only be grown successfully in areas with a moderately warm and dry climate (not more than 900 mm/35 inches per year rainfall), and on a deep permeable rich soil, preferably near to running water. Planting stock is usually unrooted sets (long cuttings) of about 3 metres length, inserted to 0.6 m. All branches should be pruned off up to a height of 2.4 m at planting and this stem should be kept free of branches by disbudding each year in the early spring as necessary. Spacing is usually 10–15 metres and rotation length 12–18 years. Cricket bat willow is not usually eligible for grant aid under the Woodland Grant Scheme.

Minor Products

Opportunities exist for marketing a number of non-timber products from woodland, such as foliage, fruit, nuts and seed, and these can often be taken advantage of at an early stage when there is no revenue to be had from timber sales.

Foliage is used extensively in floristry and species which can be marketed include eucalyptus (mainly *gunnii*), laurel, holly, Lawson cypress, western hemlock and noble fir. These can be grown as single species blocks, as coppice (only the broadleaves) to keep the height down and maximise foliage production, or as part of a mixed planting with the intention of removing the foliage component when the timber tree canopies start to affect quality of foliage.

Nuts and fruit, such as hazelnuts and damsons, can be produced from the woodland edges and rides or perimeter hedges. The cost of collection should always be borne in mind when planning to crop these minor products, as unless labour is readily available at the right time, profits will be low. Seed for propagation of forest trees is not usually produced at an early age and its production is often sporadic. If a market exists for seed then a final felling can often be timed to coincide with seed collection in a good year for seed production.

Woodland Shelter

Woodlands in Britain have been used as shelter for farm stock for centuries. Shelter is important, both for areas to overwinter and feed stock, for shade in summer and as windbreaks to shelter adjoining fields and arable crops. The importance of shelter depends on soil type, exposure and farming system, as shelter can sometimes create its own problems. On heavy soil, fields to the northern edge of woodlands can remain wet or produce reduced yields owing to the effect of shading and shelter from drying winds. Correctly designed and sited shelter, however, can enhance production and reduce costs.

In stock farming areas, particularly in exposed sites, provision of shelterbelts and shelter within existing woodlands can be very important. Shelter can reduce windspeeds and so reduce heat loss from animals in winter. Woodlands can also provide useful feeding areas which remain dry and accessible when other areas are in deep snow or suffer bad poaching damage.

It must always be remembered that grazing stock in a woodland will stop any natural regeneration and, to ensure the woodland's long-term survival, stock must be excluded at some stage to allow regeneration. This can take place in small areas at a time so that the whole woodland is regenerated over a long

PLATE 31
Traditional parkland trees may offer some shelter for livestock but have little timber value owing to heavy low branching. Timber value could be improved by pruning when young.

PLATE 32
Older stands can provide useful shelter for livestock.

period, and there is always shelter available. Grazing stock can have other damaging effects on woodland on some soil types which are prone to poaching, the roots of trees being damaged and tree growth reduced.

Two new booklets are available dealing with shelterbelts, their siting and management, one for the lowlands and one for the uplands (see Further Reading).

Reversion to Agriculture

Trees are a long-term land use and the economic circumstances at the end of a rotation are difficult to predict. The consequences of the tree crop on future agricultural use, and any effects on surrounding fields, are important and could be a consideration before deciding on the initial site to be planted.

Physical changes below a tree crop are likely to lead to an increase in soil air space, due to incorporation of leaf litter and root channels. This might be seen as an improvement to soil structure. There is often a reduction in water flow through streams in afforested areas, compared with grassland areas, but this is unlikely to be important if small blocks of woodland are planted.

In general, soil changes under a woodland rotation are unlikely to affect future agricultural use and there may be benefits in terms of improved soil structure. Stump removal will obviously be a problem for reconversion to agriculture, particularly with broadleaves, and a drainage system might have to be restored before agricultural cropping. There is, of course, a long history of conversion of woodland to agriculture with perfectly acceptable results, so only the cost of conversion and any relevant legislation regarding change of land use need influence the decision.

Further Reading

Forestry Commission publications

BULLETINS
64   *The yield of sweet chestnut coppice.*
80   *Farm woodland planning.*

LEAFLET
83   *Coppice.*

ARBORICULTURAL LEAFLET
10   *Individual tree protection.*

OCCASIONAL PAPERS
14   *The Gwent small woods project 1979–84.*
17   *Farming and forestry.*

ARBORICULTURE RESEARCH NOTE
21/80/SILS *Coppice.*

MISCELLANEOUS
Wood as fuel – a guide to burning wood efficiently.

Other publications

BARNETT, P. (1988). Shelter in the lowlands. Leaflet P MAFF/ADAS.
BRONWIN, A. (1988). Shelterbelts in the uplands. Leaflet P3154. MAFF/ADAS.
NATURE CONSERVANCY COUNCIL. *Hedges and shelterbelts.* NCC Booklet E1.2.
NATIONAL FARMERS' UNION (1986). *Farming trees – the case for government support for woodland on farms.* NFU Policy Document.
STOTT, K.G., McELROY, G., ABERNETHY, W. AND HAYES, D.P. (1985). *Coppice willow for biomass in the UK.* Long Ashton Research Station, Bristol.

Appendix

Useful Addresses

Arboricultural Association
Ampfield House
Ampfield
Nr ROMSEY
Hants
SO51 9PA
Tel: 0794 68717

Association of Professional Foresters
Brokerswood House
Brokerswood
Nr WESTBURY
Wiltshire
BA13 4EH
Tel: 0373 822238

British Timber Merchants' Association (England & Wales)
Ridgeway House
6 Ridgeway Road
Long Ashton
BRISTOL
BS18 9EU
Tel: 0272 394022

Countryside Commission (England & Wales)
John Dower House
Crescent Place
CHELTENHAM
Gloucestershire
GL50 3RA
Tel: 0242 521381

Countryside Commission for Scotland
Battleby
Redgorton
PERTH
PH1 3EW
Tel: 0738 27921

Home Timber Merchants
Association of Scotland
16 Gordon Street
GLASGOW
G1 3QE
Tel: 041 221 6551

Institute of Chartered Foresters
22 Walker Street
EDINBURGH
EH3 7HR
Tel: 031 225 2705

Nature Conservancy Council
Northminster House
PETERBOROUGH
PE1 1UA
Tel: 0733 40345

Nature Conservancy Council
12 Hope Terrace
EDINBURGH
EH9 2AS
Tel: 031 447 4784

Royal Forestry Society of England, Wales & Northern Ireland
102 High Street
TRING
Hertfordshire
HP23 4AH
Tel: 044 282 2028

Royal Scottish Forestry Society
11 Atholl Crescent
EDINBURGH
EH3 8HE
Tel: 031 229 8180

The Tree Council
35 Belgrave Square
LONDON
SW1X 8NQ
Tel: 01 235 8854

Timber Growers United Kingdom
Agriculture House
Knightsbridge
LONDON
SW1X 7NJ
Tel: 01 235 2925

Timber Growers United Kingdom
5 Dublin Street Lane South
EDINBURGH
EH1 3PX
Tel: 031 557 0944

Woodland Trust
Autumn Park
Dysart Road
GRANTHAM
Lincs
NG31 6LL
Tel: 0476 74297

Addresses of ADAS, DAFS, DANI and WOAD regional offices
are given in the local telephone directory.

Index

Printed in the United Kingdom for Her Majesty's Stationery Office
Dd 290513   C 70   6/88